Odet

2 0 1 7
Vol. I

EDITOR IN CHIEF	Laura Kepner
MANAGING EDITOR	Warren Firschein
ART DIRECTOR	Carrie Granato
POETRY EDITORS	Nancy Bruckner
	Barbara Finkelstein
	Deb Klein
NONFICTION EDITOR	Nicole Caron
FICTION EDITORS	Amy Bryant
	Warren Firschein
	Carrie Granato
CONTRIBUTING EDITOR	Chris Shaun

Published Jointly by

SAFETY HARBOR WRITERS & POETS
CHAPTER TWO PRESS

Odet is published annually. Visit our website, www.theodet.com, for full submission guidelines and deadlines. Email submissions to OdetJournal@gmail.com or mail to Odet Journal, c/o Chapter Two Press, P.O. Box 870, Safety Harbor, FL 34695. No query can be answered unless accompanied by a stamped, self-addressed envelope or submitted electronically.

Printed in the United States of America
Cover photography by Alaina Virgilio
Cover design by Carrie Granato
The text type was set in Plantin

VOLUME ONE • 2017

Odet

To our Readers 5

Janet Watson	*From Hand to Hand* 7
Daniela Gutierrez	*Burial Mounds* 9
Jason Swierk	*Ancient Tides* 11
Maureen Jenkins	*Rose Garden in the Cemetery* 15
Darla Klein **	*Withlacoochee Holiday* 16
Lennie Hay	*Sentinel* 19
Janet Watson	*A Day on Old Tampa Bay* 20
Resie Waechter	*Swamp Life* 21
Elisa Silverstein	*Blurry Branches* 24
Wendy Keppley	*Growing up in "The Garden Spot"* 25
Noah Snitzer	*Harmony* 28
Gregory Byrd	*Deer Hunting in the Everglades* 29
Andrea McBride	*La Tortuga* 33
Jeff Jeter	*Snipe Tipping* 34
Cheryl A. Van Beek	*Winter Garden* 35
Carrie Granato	*On Hoover's Trail* 37
Jaclyn Telfair	*The Rattlesnake* 41
Jen Karetnick *	*At Riverbend Park* 45
Romeo Lemay	*PAR* 47
Marcia Morley	*1967* 50
Katherine Kennedy	*The Cove* 51
Marcia Morley **	*Inverness* 55
P. R. King	*Magical Florida* 57
Deborah Klein	*The Belle's View* 59
Walt Belcher	*Memories of Trains Gone By* 65
Amy Bryant	*I Am the Voice* .68
Camilla Shoosmith	*Sun Worn* 70

Dianne Persall — *The Race* ... 71
Cameron Hunt McNabb ★ — *Threads* ... 73
Katherine Nichols — *The Big Guava* ... 78
Michelle Glans — *Viva Ybor* ... 79
William Willard — *Balance Sheet* ... 81
Elyse Thomas — *Palm Trees* ... 82
Brooks Peters — *Pilgrimage* ... 83
Patricia Daharsh — *Ahead of Her Time* ... 85
Lennie Hay — *Life Lines* ... 89
Kaitlin Murphy-Knudsen ★★ — *Heat* ... 93
Vivian Taylor — *Roadside Teddy Bear Shrine* ... 99
Louise Moses — *After the Summer Flowers* ... 100
Warren Firschein — *The Skull* ... 101
Chino Rolon — *Express Yourself* ... 107

Photographers:

Holly Apperson — *Baranoff Oak* ... 10
Bruce Duncan — *Noble Egret* ... 18
Laurie Ross — *Untitled* ... 40
Terrie Dahl Thomas — *Untitled* ... 46, 64
Alaina Virgilio — *Ybor City* ... 80

CONTRIBUTORS ... 111

★   First Prize Winner, 2016 Romeo Lemay Writing Contest
★★   Second Prize Winner, 2016 Romeo Lemay Writing Contest

To our Readers:

The journal is named for the man we consider to be Safety Harbor's first storyteller: Odet (oh-day) Philippe, who moved to the area in the 1840s and is credited with the development of citrus and cigar industries. Philippe is remembered as a count of noble birth, a childhood friend of Napoleon who later served as his chief surgeon, and a friend of pirates. He may have told such tales to disguise his past and elevate his status, or to simply amuse his grandchildren. Whatever the truth, we do know that he was a generous man, whose life has become legendary, and that legend intrigues us, especially the stories that survived him.

The idea to publish coincided with an annual contest in honor of a fellow writer and beloved friend, Romeo Lemay, an original member of Safety Harbor Writers & Poets. After his passing in 2013, Romeo's son Tim offered to fund a writing contest in his dad's name. We opened the contest to all of Florida and the results pleasantly surprised us. Winning entries are included in the following pages. We have also included *PAR*, a story by Romeo from his self-published book, *Facts, Fiction, Fantasies and Foolishness*. I remember Romeo's French Canadian accent as he read his stories aloud. Like many of the contributors to this journal, his stories commemorate the people who came before us, and as we hope you will notice, also honor the state many of us did not grow up in, but have adopted with an intense love of home.

For this, our first edition, we chose to honor Florida. We were thrilled to receive submissions that touched upon many phases and attributes that have inspired generations: its history, beauty, wildlife, and community, from the early days of pottery making to the destruction of beloved landmarks.

The editors of *Odet* hope you enjoy this inaugural issue and welcome your feedback. For details on future submissions, visit www.theodet.com.

Happy reading!

Laura Kepner
OdetJournal@gmail.com

Janet Watson

From Hand to Hand
a tribute to the ancient makers of Safety Harbor ware

The old ones have left their legacies
of stone and bone
to those of us who believe we see
their shadows fishing in the bay,
their children digging
along the shore.

To touch a thing of the past—
a finely-crafted arrowhead
or a sewing tool, is to value
the vision of the maker
and the intent of the user
who once lived in this place.
The years between their time
and ours fall away.

Artifacts transcending necessity
connect us in a human desire
for beauty in design.
The outline of a hand
grasps the curve
of a sand-tempered bowl
and reaches across centuries
to touch us and remind us
that the potter's hand
was once warm flesh.

Yesterday she was. Today I am.
Under the same blanket of sky,
beside this basin of blue water
where I so often walk,
she slept and dreamed,
awakened to work, and,
unaware that I would be here,
she left something behind for me.

Daniela Gutierrez

Burial Mounds

I. Body
Rip it apart, limb by
limb—now, don't be shy.
Separate it, and into
the jars it goes.

II. Bones
The flesh must be
removed from
the bones over the
course of two days,
tearing it like
wet leaves.

Be wary of cougars
for they are hungry and
wary of none.

III. Skeleton
Slip it together, bone
to bone interlocking
into the marvelous puzzle
born of intention.

For four days, we fast
for he can eat no more.

IV. Burial Mound
Now, we lay him
to his final rest.
Let him sleep, enveloped
by the darkness.

Baranoff Oak, *Holly Apperson*

Jason Swierk

Ancient Tides

One last heave across the scratchy sand and the nose of the canoe slides into the bay. Without a sound, bare feet hop from beach to shallows, then in a smooth arc, Acu twists his hip over the side of the dugout and lands facing me with a grin.

We drift out past the mangroves, his body tense and motionless, listening. A roaring fire, visible over his shoulder, illuminates the village women's gyrating bodies, the rustling of their palmetto skirts muffled by men in deerskin breechcloths encircling them.

I shiver. Not from the night air wrapping me in its thick, steamy embrace, but the excitement of escaping. Breaking the rules, like we did when we were younger. Back when we weren't old enough to be out on the water by ourselves.

We aren't forbidden to see each other, but the judging stares and guarded whispers are enough for us to hide our friendship. It happened gradually, the rest of the village children our age separating, girls out picking grapes and boys learning to hunt and fish, then going off together, while Acu and I continued to find each other.

How often had we sat under the mossy trees, Acu sharing what he'd learned about bows and spears? As with most things in my life, I can't be sure if the villagers treat me differently and remain silent because I'm Chief Tocobaga's daughter or because I lost my mother at such a young age.

Whatever the reason, I'm happy the ceremony has allowed us to slip away unnoticed. When the fire disappears behind the mangroves, my eyes adjust to the softer glow of the moonlight spreading across the bay, the transformation giving me a better view of his face. His eyes, sharp and focused on me, quickly turn away.

He reaches for the paddle in the bottom of the canoe and dips it into the calm surface, propelling us farther along the shore. Sounds of the ceremony fade, replaced by the curls of water behind his steady strokes. His apparent fear at meeting my gaze denies me another glimpse at the curious look in his eyes when I caught him staring.

I used to laugh when he'd draw thin red lines diagonally across his soft cheeks like the men preparing for war, but sitting across from me now, jaw set, with the permanent tattoos of a warrior streaking his face, arms, and chest, he feels different. Powerful. Dangerous.

A twinge rises from my stomach to my own unadorned chest, free of tattoos, but changed in other ways and exposed in the humid air, betraying me. He stops paddling and we drift in silence, each lost in our own thoughts. We've always shared everything, but now I feel, like me, he has secrets. Secrets I want to know.

The next morning when the sun rises over the bay, I sit on the edge of the mound where father's house rises above the shore and watch the villagers move around the plaza below. Oak trees, moss hanging from their branches, shield wide open blue skies, and the hot sun reflects off the water, unchanged from yesterday. But, something is different, vibrating.

Out of the corner of my eye, I see unfamiliar canoes approaching and run into the house to warn father. He charges down the ramp and the plaza is swarmed by villagers.

Men scramble for spears and bows, racing to the water's edge. Acu, normally sitting next to me to watch the Calusa attack from the safety of the mound, instead grabs his own bow and sprints to the shore. Toward danger. My stomach sinks at the thought of him returning injured, possibly dead, another pile of bones in the temple mound across the plaza from where I sit.

He's fast and reaches the water ahead of many grown men and crouches in the brush, waiting. As the canoes near the shore, I notice something strange. Not all these men are Calusa. Some are lighter skinned with dark hair growing on their faces. Like animals.

When they come ashore, the pale men lead, Calusa following behind. I'd never seen men like these before, but remember childhood stories of another chief's daughter saving one of them from death, falling in love with him. My lips pinch in disgust. I could never love one of these course, ugly men, bodies hidden under strange coverings, weak and unsightly next to the robust men of the village and Calusa glistening in their deerskin breechcloths.

Hours later, scanning the assembled crowd in the plaza, I catch Acu looking up at me. He smiles and stands, making his way up the mound. Dirty from hiding in the brush, but not bloody, not dead, he sits beside me.

"You can't be up here," I say. "We'll be caught."

"They're too busy to notice," he says. "Talking about a treaty."

"With the Calusa?"

"And the pale men," he says.

I'm not sure what to say. What to think.

"I don't trust them," he says. "Those pale men. Each time they come there are more of them."

I'm shocked. "You've seen them before?"

"No, just heard the stories, like you."

Relieved there aren't more secrets he's keeping from me, I stare down at the men. They do look dangerous. The way they landed the canoes, crushing the vegetation and stomping their way into the plaza with their heavy boots. Aggressive, destructive. Worse than the Calusa.

"I'm glad you didn't have to fight," I say.

His eyes soften and he searches me with more intensity. That look again. It feels like he's touching me and I get the urge to be closer. Without thinking, I reach out and wrap my fingers around his arm and press my lips to his. I don't know why I do it, I just know I want to. There's a rush, like the creek after a strong rain, flooding out into the bay. It feels like telling him my secrets in a way I could never do with words.

He rests a hand on my hip and gently draws me in. There is nothing else in the world, but the two of us. Our bodies. His hands. Not the playful hands of a boy, the strong hands of a man.

Suddenly, he stops, pulls back. Without a word, he stands and makes his way back down the ramp.

Days pass and I see Acu down in the plaza a few times, but Father has forbidden me from leaving the mound and Acu refuses to look up. As the sun starts to set I see him sharpening the point of an atlatl and listen for my father's nearby voice leading a meeting of the elders before heading down the ramp. Acu turns with a start.

His face darkens. "You can't be here."

"I want to talk to you."

"No."

"Are you mad at me?"

Something flickers in his eyes. Something he wants to hide. But he can't hide from me, I know him too well. I grab his arm and hold it firm.

He tries to pull away, but not hard enough for me to lose my grasp. For a brief moment, I think of the innocent boy I could often overpower if I set my mind to it, but this time it wasn't my strength holding him back.

"I don't want them to hurt you," he says.

"Hurt me? Why would they hurt me?"

Then I think about it. I am the chief's daughter. If they were to take me, to force me . . ."

Sensing my distress, he rests his hand on my shoulder. "Not just you. They will harm all of us."

He is right. I can feel it. Why did I think they would soon leave, that my father would be able to deny them what they wanted like he'd done with the Calusa in the past? That we'd be able to go back to the way things were before.

Acu looks down at me. "They will take what is ours."

His words, cold and possessive, make me shiver.

"What can we do?" I ask.

"Kill them, like our fathers did with that priest years ago."

I flinch at the thought. Not the slaughter of our enemies, but the number of Tocobaga that would die. Maybe Father. Maybe Acu. And this wasn't some defenseless priest, this was the Calusa, the tribe we've been at war with since before I was born. The tribe that has come close to overrunning us without the help of these pale men.

When I speak I don't even realize I've done it out loud. "We can't win."

He starts to protest, but I move my hand farther up his arm. "No, Acu."

He relaxes under my touch, our shared past enough for him to accept my words.

"I want to protect you," he says. "Protect this place, protect our home, even if I have to give up my own life."

When his eyes meet mine with that same curious gaze from the canoe, I am no longer confused. Steady and penetrating, his desire flows over me like the changing tides, forcing me to accept that life will never be the same. To accept that we are different now, he and I, no longer children, but the next generation of our people.

Maureen Jenkins

Rose Garden in the Cemetery

When we first went there close to dusk in late November—
Slowly moving between tombstones
A step here a step there

        between two trees blowing leaves
        cut off from most breathing humans:

shuffling towards lake in the cemetery
past the All American Beauty rose garden—

        serenity and gate to Paradise.

fish break the water
alligator sign looms nearby
off in distance a coyote watches our every move.

        A woman in a green overcoat
snaps pictures of the Iceberg Rose and Coral Princess.

        Living humans seeking refuge.

Darla Klein

Withlacoochee Holiday

Water skimmers sparkle
in a no wake zone.

Cypress knees like
hitching posts
wait at river's edge
enough for a herd of
riverhorses, if our guests
should arrive that way.

(Just pullin' your leg, see.)

Trees trimmed with
Spanish moss emit
a sumptuous air.

Where the banks lie far apart
beds of flowers line our
liquid driveway
opposite islands
of water lilies.

Anhingas shimmer
on rocks, gators
lounge
on logs.

ODET

When visitors ask
about swimmin',
like this is Disney,
we tell 'em, "Oh, it's safe
anywhere, but not always."

The land's edge is even
with the water, but they
don't mingle.

This is the South;
the river minds his manners.

Noble Egret, *Bruce Duncan*

18

Sentinel

Fragile
      sleek white body
         spindle leg
            needle-sharp beak
               mask a stoic's heart.

                  Pin-hole eyes like a magnet
            hold and pierce ours,
        empty cottage, dingy glass
and memory.

He stands erect,
certain of his work,
confronts
our doubt.

Silent in the sun's cycle
         he faces puffs of humid
           gulf breath
              tantrum waves.
                  He wades, he watches.

                Satisfied with
           found fish
        ready food from friends
      he wades, he watches,
    trusts the earth rhythms
blue above, blue below.

He stands on one leg,
protects his warmth,
clutches it close
to his Heron heart.
He waits.

Janet Watson

A Day on Old Tampa Bay

North of the noise, beyond the bridges,
kayaks and paddleboards skim
across their own reflections.
Land-creatures who paddle forth,
easing onto this water-world
as though they approach a high altar,
receive the blessing of a breeze.
Cloud mountains, templed in the bluest of skies,
float above these innocent crafts.

Fearlessly, dolphin and manatee
swim beneath and around them.
Where no motors churn and no blades slice,
they cavort in joyful welcome
and recognize a kinship with those
who tread on solid earth
but find solace in the liquid silver
that ripples off their quiet paddles.

A brown pelican wings through the salty air,
and its feathered cousins, on lanky legs,
stalk the mudflats slowly. They appear
as rooted as the mangroves,
in gentle communion with the sea.
Eelgrass sways in the shallows. Time stills.
The paddlers hold their breaths
in the beauty of the moment—
sunrise, noon and sunset merging.

Swamp Life

I fell in love with orchids unexpectedly while crossing one of the required books off of our class reading list. Learning about old Florida life, Native American history, and people's obsession with plants, I shoved the book—now full of dog-eared pages and underlined sentences that made my breath catch in my throat—into my wife's hands and told her that today she needed to start reading this book, and that today we needed to go out and buy an orchid from the local garden center so that I would never forget how this writing made me feel.

She did start reading the book, and we did go out and buy an orchid that day. It was beautiful and wild-looking and sexy, and I explained to Stephanie that the publishers of *The Orchid Thief* had trouble finding a picture of an orchid for the cover that wasn't too overtly sexual. We laughed at this as I placed the orchid on my dresser and, at the advice of the grower I inquired, laid an ice cube in its pot.

Stephanie was only a few chapters into the book when we drove down to South Florida to explore the Fakahatchee Strand, but it didn't matter. Even without reading up on it beforehand, it would take a lot for someone to be able to jump into the freezing cold swamp water, PVC pipe-turned-walking-stick in hand, and look around without feeling small and insignificant and absolutely amazed at what Mother Nature is capable of creating.

I was almost hesitant to love orchids so much. I fell hard and fast and I was fully aware of how cliché that was, considering the fact that we were reading a book about crazy passionate "orchid people" in class. But the book was about more than a flower; it was about an entire species, a life force, a perseverance. *The Orchid Thief* is about falling in love and getting your heart broken, about being misunderstood, about nearly dying so many times that even you yourself are shocked to be getting back up and breathing again. I guess that's what made me fall for the orchid: it reminded me of all of the bad things, and all of the good things, that I have ever done in my life. It made me feel guilty and it made me feel proud, but most of all, it made me want to keep going.

The plant I picked out was white and plain for an orchid. I felt shy and maybe a little embarrassed, even, to be purchasing it. I didn't want to be the person that fell in love with them and bought a bunch and enjoyed them for a little while, only to forget about them and let them die on my windowsill, later thrown in the trash and picked up by the City on a random Tuesday in June. I also didn't want to be the person that Susan Orlean mentions over and over in her book, the one that spends every spare cent on orchids, on breeding them and blending them and raising them and selling them. Part of me got angry reading about all of the people who tried to "play God" with their plants, creating hybrids and species that will live longer than their great-grandchildren and bear the family name for generations to come. It feels egotistical to name a plant species after yourself, and I attempted to sift through the names of the different flowers to make sure I wasn't buying into that.

Ultimately, Stephanie and I settled on an orchid plant apiece. Mine was tall and white, the petals of which reminded me of faces tilted up towards the sky to sing with the sun. Stephanie picked a speckled bunch, purple and white with random bits of orange. They were so spectacular that they were almost obvious, except that their sloppy splotches looked careless and accidental, and I am guessing that's the only reason so many of them remained in stock. We tended to our flowers and caught up on our reading as we prepared for our trip through the Swamp. The weeks rushed by and we didn't know what to expect. It had been quite some time since we'd stormed through the elements together.

Trudging through the sap and sludge, my feet were freezing and my eyes were bright. I was tired and hungry and glad I didn't have that extra glass or two of pinot grigio last night after all; this is not the place one wants to suffer through a hangover. The high-pitched squeals of girls several yards behind me made me grateful that I'm not twenty-two anymore, and the booming enthusiasm of our swamp biologist escort Mike both humbled and inspired me. The palms brought me back to my study abroad hikes through the Belizean rainforest; the spectacle of a gator eating a heron brought me back to the trek I took through Payne's Prairie with my brothers last summer, and now I was looking at something even more extraordinary: the fledgling roots of an endangered orchid—barely there, barely noticeable, but existing and present and alive.

Had our biologist Mike not pointed them out, I would never have seen the wild orchid roots dangling there on the pine tree branches, even though there were several of them. They were so tiny and delicate and responsible for keeping the existence of their entire species intact that I was almost afraid to be too close to them, with my big eyes and loud clumsiness. These orchids aren't endangered because of any other animal but us, and I found myself muttering a weak and silent apology to them for being a part of that. I cringed every time someone brushed past the lowest branch, trying to warn each classmate that *this* was the tree Mike was talking about, and *those* were the branches he was referring to. Our bulky, tired steps made our way back to the road and I tried not to look back, knowing I wouldn't be able to see the roots from this distance.

Leaving the green shelter of the swamp, our group stepped back up onto the gravelly road and made our way back to our vehicles. A few of the girls stopped when they saw me pointing out another flower on the side of the road, its long white petals in full bloom. "Is it another alligator?!" a fellow student squealed. "No," replied someone else, "it's another orchid in bloom."

"Pfffffffft." She stuck out her tongue and rolled her heavily-made-up eyes. "I am *so* sick of orchids."

Blurry Branches

My dark limbs create a blurred shadow on the floor.
A light fog wraps herself around me,
my darkness seeping through her.
She loses herself
And I catch her as her tears rain down on me.
Time picks her up,
and she's dancing around me.
Here I sit in this humid skin,
waiting for her to fall
and love me again.

Wendy Keppley

Growing up in "The Garden Spot"

I gazed past my friend's face and saw the familiar three bumps on top of the water. Two hooded eyes and the tip of a triangular snout surfaced about thirty yards away, signaling that several more gators would soon appear, taking over our spot in the lake.

This always happened at the end of the day. I curled my toes, squishing the muck below my feet, standing shoulder deep in Little Lake Jackson with my best friend, Alandee. The water remained warm even as the sun was sinking beneath the edge of the horizon.

"Are you going to Teen Town tomorrow night?" I asked. Behind her, the gator's head disappeared underneath the water. "I'm thinking that new guy might be there with Jimmy and Marty."

"Maybe we should. I heard Bobby is going." A teasing smile lit up her face.

Alandee lived next door and we often spent hours in the water. Already having played "King of the Raft" with our little brothers, Geoff and Brad, we were tired of dunking them and winning. So we escaped their shrieks and splash attacks by going deeper into the lake, out of their reach.

My parents, who were raised in Wisconsin until they followed their hearts and moved to Florida as a young married couple, had taught me what they considered to be the cardinal rule upon entering the lake at the edge of our property. As I walked through cat-tails towards deeper water, I had to splash around me in order to scare things away. Things like snakes, garfish, snapping turtles, and alligators. Oh, and I wasn't supposed to throw marshmallows in the water to feed the alligators, as Mr. Mac, our old neighbor next door, often did. My parents didn't like that too much.

But now, our fun came to an end as usual when my mother yelled. "Kids, look around, the sun is setting. It's time to come in to shore now."

My folks usually walked down to the lake after Dad got home from work. They liked to relax, sometimes in their beach chairs, other times sitting on the raft. We pushed through from deep to shallow water and finally emerged onto damp sand.

"What's for dinner?" I asked.

"See ya'll later," Alandee said as she and Geoff grabbed their towels and ran home for supper.

Years later, I learned that many people, in fact most people, did not swim alongside alligators. How, I wondered, had my loving parents ever allowed their twelve-year-old daughter to swim with gators?

My parents were reliable, but one time my mother did not show up at the bus stop as expected. In the sixth grade, she always picked me up a half mile down from our house. A day came, though, when I stepped off the bus and didn't see her car. The sun was beating down, making the thought of walking home seem impossible. Nevertheless, I was hungry, and realized I had no other choice. I started my journey, a pre-adolescent seething with the indignity of having to endure such a hardship.

I paced through the heat, perspiring, and angrier with each step. Finally, I stomped through the side door, hot, sweaty and fuming as only a wronged child can. Mom stood in the middle of our patio, still as a statue, staring at a huge alligator as he glided lazily down the small canal in our back yard. "Shh," she said. "Just watch. Isn't he something?"

I joined her. It was calming to see the gator swim by and my anger drained away as my mother and I appreciated the majestic creature go about his life. We stood side by side in silence until the remarkable animal disappeared behind the distant cattails. Then my stomach rumbled and I dashed into the kitchen to raid the fridge, going about my life as usual.

My older sister sometimes told me stories about being bundled up in warm coats, mittens and a hat, just to step outside in the snow. She also told me how happy Mom and Dad were to move down to Florida, even though it had been a huge step for them to leave behind their home, family, and friends. So we both knew that our parents lived in gratitude that they could raise their family in a natural, healthy, and warm place of beauty. Mom and Dad often called our place "the Garden Spot of America."

I believed in the rules my parents had about wild creatures and learned to approach life with a strong confidence that if I did what was right, everything would be alright. I also learned to value all living things. This respect for life extended to the people and community around me. Later, I learned I was fortunate and somewhat unique to grow up in Florida without fear of gators and snakes.

My family ate dinner together as usual that night, sharing pot roast, red potatoes, corn on the cob, sliced white Sunbeam bread, real butter, and Borden's whole milk. After dessert, all six of us, aged three to adult, played "I

Spy" and told jokes around our dining table. The round table, all the way from the Maas Brothers department store in Tampa, was inlaid with bamboo leaves and small seashells, and it still remains in our family. The laughter drowned out the drone of our new black and white television, ever-present during dinner hour.

As years passed, I tuned in enough to hear the daily news with Huntley and Brinkley, the news my parents didn't want to miss, which was the daily casualty count of the Vietnam War.

I remember one night, after the death toll was announced, it upset me more than usual. After all, I was sixteen then, with a nineteen-year-old boyfriend. I turned to my folks and asked, "Mom, Dad? Hey, do you think John's selective service number is high enough? What if he gets drafted?"

"He's going to college in the fall, so he will be okay. He's lucky he had that choice," was all Dad said.

"Eat your ice cream. Do you want Hershey's chocolate syrup on top?" Mom added, smoothly distracting me.

I grew up in a small town in Florida, during an age of bomb drills where we crawled under our desks to protect ourselves from nuclear fallout. Around me swirled the turbulence of the times: the women's lib movement, peace sit-ins, the shootings at Kent State, hippies, and the political assassinations of Robert Kennedy, President John F. Kennedy, and Martin Luther King.

But through it all, I shared my parents' appreciation for the outdoors. I reveled in the clear blue skies, green grass almost year-round, short trips to visit the ocean and always, living near the silver lake. Of course the challenges of school, our church youth group, and scouting activities kept me busy and growing. I thrived in a happy bubble of childhood safety and fun in a warm and beautiful place, all because my parents envisioned a better place to raise a family and followed their dream.

With love and determination, my parents were somehow able to shield their young from the events unfolding around them. And, while they did let me swim in a lake full of weeds, snakes, snapping turtles, garfish, and gators, they taught me how to splash before entering and always, always to respect sundown, when the alligators came alive.

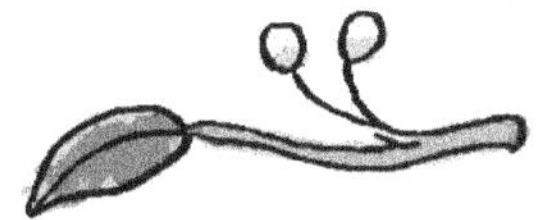

Harmony

Water ripples as the pulses of living creatures
croon as one to the morning sun.
A frog slips soundlessly below the surface
as the volume of Spanish words
rise beyond the cattails and hanging vines.
Two fisherman drift by on a wooden raft
and lay peacefully with the waking spoonbills
as they dry their blushing feathers
on the Tampa Bay coast.

Gregory Byrd

Deer Hunting in the Everglades

I had fished with my father since I was three years old. In Key Largo, in 1968, my parents were living as caretakers of a weekend house owned by a bank in Miami. My mother would clean the "big house," wash the linens, dust, clean the floors, make the beds, and get it back in shape after the reveling or relaxing of the past weekend. She would cut the weedy grass that grew out of the rocky yard there. My father had a job putting up antennas. With the stipend they got from cleaning the house and keeping watch on things and my father's paycheck, there wasn't a whole lot to keep things going for a couple with one toddler and a new infant (my sister). So when my father took me fishing, it was for food. We rowed out into a Florida Bay more pristine than it is now, and we would catch snapper and grunts and my father would then filet them and freeze them in bags of ice. When he got a boat, I fished with him far out into the Gulf Stream, where I landed a big kingfish when I was about eight. As I grew up, I grew to know the ways of fish, how fish ate one another, how crabs and scavenger fish would clean the carcass of dead fish, how birds would carry away anything that floated. I learned all this with so much subtlety that there was never any sort of initiation into fishing. But my father had never taken me hunting until I was thirteen.

While I had certainly been blooded by fishing early on (I caught and cleaned my own fish by the time I was eight) I had no idea about hunting deer. When I was about twelve, we visited my grandparents' farm on my mother's side and, while we were there, they butchered a heifer. I watched as my uncle, grandfather and my dad loaded the .38 and walked out the door. Although I was a gentle kid and loved animals, I wanted to watch, probably just to be with the men. But my father—wisely I understand now—made me stay inside the little house with my mother and grandmother where I listened for the gunshot. The men weren't happy or sad when they came in. They were businesslike, doing the gruesome work of a farm, but there was some dark kinship among them. Maybe it was with some memory of this that my father called his friend Bill Waddell the following year and planned a deer hunting trip to the Everglades.

The week before the trip, we went over to Bill and Blanche's house to look at Bill's guns. Bill had served in the army at some point, in something talked about only in hushed tones, perhaps Special Forces or something like that. From his closet, he took a big, dangerous-looking black .45 automatic, dropped the clip, cleared the chamber and let me hold it. It was not the same experience as I'd imagined as I saw Sgt. York or John Wayne brandish the same weapon. I placed the heavy gun on the bed. Then Bill pulled a lever action .30-.30 like cowboys used, a pump shotgun and a carbine like they carried in *Combat!* on Saturday afternoons. I was to carry the carbine, which was placed in my hands. I wrapped my hands around the wood of the stock, made sure the safety was in place and gently fingered the trigger. I sighted down the barrel to a lamp at the edge of the room. I knew a little already about guns. I'd owned a Daisy air rifle since I was eight and had, to my credit, dozens of tin cans and the first rat discovered in our garage, which in a suicidal display, had walked out of the clutter and stopped immediately below the bullseye I had painted on an old box I was using as a target. I had lowered the rifle and fired, leveling the animal.

Every night that week, I talked with my dad about hunting deer, about where to shoot, about what it would all be like. I imagined Dan'l Boone sorts of scenes, of my picture next to a hanging fourteen-point buck. Then the day came when we loaded the guns and the sleeping bags and cans of Dinty Moore Beef Stew into my dad's Ford panel van and we headed north to the Everglades on a Friday afternoon. The road into the hunting area was mostly a rutted limestone path used by Jeeps and other four-wheelers and the van bounced uncomfortably until we finally found a place to park. We heated the stew over a little fire and drank coffee with dried creamer in it. After dinner, I stood outside with my dad and Bill while they passed a flask filled with Wild Turkey. It was cold out there—close to freezing—and I stamped my feet like they did and took a sip of the whiskey which my dad said would keep me warm but which burned even before I could taste much of it. They laughed and slapped me on the back. As dusk faded, mosquitoes began to come out in earnest. More than just slapping one or two, they came in swarms like in *The African Queen*. My father said something to Bill about his smoking keeping mosquitoes away. Then, my father, who had quit a heavy smoking habit cold turkey ten years ago, lit up one of Bill's cigarettes in order to keep the mosquitoes away. I watched my dad with the cigarette in his mouth, looking far off at something as he drew the smoke into his lungs. He looked like someone from a movie of who he was before he ever had me, of who he was when he was an Air Force policeman in Reno, maybe, when he was single a long time before me. Then he turned to me and blew a steady stream of smoke from my head all down my body. The mosquitoes lifted from me for a moment and he repeated the act until he had finished his cigarette. It had started to drizzle and the longer we stood in the cold, the more the drizzle turned to rain than ran down my ball cap. We escaped into the van, where we dried off and swatted the mosquitoes that came in with us. We bedded down on the musty olive drab sleeping bags and I drifted to sleep, listening to Bill snore loudly, the rain on the metal roof, and automatic gunfire and growling swamp buggies in the distance. I dreamed of fleet brown deer that night.

In the morning, we had more coffee and the men primed me on how the hunt would go. They would fan out to the sides and I would walk down the middle. If a deer was flushed, I was to have first shot and to be careful what I shot at. The paths we walked were wet, and we stepped on chunks of limestone. The rising sun burned the mosquitoes away and soon we could no longer see our breaths.

On the rocks, we walked up on pygmy rattlesnakes coiled and working hard to wring whatever warmth they could from the rocks and the rising sun so they could go on their own hunts. I expected my father to warn me about them, or to tell me to shoot them, to say something. He had always warned me from danger or from being a danger to other people, but now I only sensed him waiting behind me. Bill said nothing. It seemed like the Everglades was listening while I stood there with my carbine, more lethal than I had ever been. I waited for them to rattle or bolt as we came near, but they only lifted their heads a bit. Venomous enough to kill a boy or old man or put him into the hospital, they were now cold and helpless. I thought of not having killed anything yet. I thought of rattlers I'd seen skinned out or made into belts or hatbands. I eased the safety and nudged one with the muzzle of my rifle. It moved its rattler weakly. I re-set the safety on my rifle and, instead of stepping around the rattler, I stepped over it, and it remained coiled. I stepped over the others there on the cold trail and the men followed, said nothing. As far as we walked that day, we saw no deer and no other game.

The van had sunk to its axles in mud the night before and needed to be pulled out by Jeep. When even a passing Jeep couldn't free it, my father walked to the nearest bar and hunting lodge for a swamp buggy. While he was gone, I fired Bill's .22 pistol into a paper plate target. That was the only gun I fired that day. I hadn't killed anything. On the way home in the van, I drank coffee with them men and carved a deer out of a piece of wood I'd found, making a totem of the lesson I thought I'd missed.

Andrea McBride

La Tortuga

Underneath a wide-brimmed hat,
the woman squints
at something in the distance.
She points and asks, "What is?"
I want to reply, "la tortuga."
The Spanish climbs into my mouth
when I hear her accent.
Instead "turtle" tumbles
from my tongue sounding dumber.
I watch the rubbery head crown,
then recede
into its bony shell of a home.

Snipe Tipping

As young newlyweds
We'd often go camping
Ocala, Myakka and Saint Augustine
The blood we had thinned
Mosquitoes were sapping
Dirt in her hairdo and holes in my jeans

We gathered dry branches
That littered the forest
Armloads of needles and palmetto fans
Crickets, cicadas
Like Caroline chorus
Aluminum taters and beans from a can

Saturday nights
Soon slip into Sundays
Dismantle the bedroom and piss out the fire
Back to bulb lights
And civilization
Toilets, warm water and telephone wire

Isaac, my son
Let's go snipe hunting
Before Daddy's monsters are all dead and gone
Crazy as sin
Cute as a button
His nightmare she's dreaming
He's screaming her song

Cheryl A. Van Beek

Winter Garden

There's a freeze warning—no chorus of frogs
singing in our Florida forest tonight.
They're nestled in the muddy bottom of the pond.
The army of fire ants that normally patrols
our yard is asleep in the barracks below.

Arms heaped with enough gauzy white sheets
to stage a Halloween fright fest,
my husband and I charge into our yard
pivoting our flashlights like a search party.
We stomp our feet hoping the vibrations
ward off cottonmouths seeking warmth in our garden beds.

Frost cloth flaps like winter flags in the wind,
snapping back at us as we try to cover
all the pentas and hibiscus we bought last summer.
Startled by a roar of scraping and clanking,
we glance at each other wide eyed, then look around.
My flashlight shines on the culprit—
it glares at us with glowing eyes.

An armadillo is wedged between
the viburnum and our compressor. It drags
its shell along cement, clatters
against the air conditioner.
Disturbed by our flashlights and chatter,
it wriggles its rabbit-like ears at us
before dashing to our neighbor's porch for some peace.

Back to stretching and stapling fabric,
flashlights roll away, pegs slip through our stiff fingers.
With a couple of hours and duct tape,
we've finally pieced together
a patchwork quilt of protection.

On Hoover's Trail

There are two things I know to be true this very moment: I am marrying not only Jake, but his dog Hoover; and Hoover and I are irrevocably lost.

We are trapped in the middle of a marshy woodland that isn't even noble enough to be considered a swamp. What started out as a romantic camping trip has turned into a bad *Survivor* rerun faster than a mosquito's bite.

I swat at yet another bloodsucker, but it flies away laughing as I smack my neck. I wish I could kick myself for trying to prove I am what I am not.

I'm not a dog person.

Hoover cocks his tongue-lolling head at me as if I have thought the unfathomable.

"What? So I'm not a dog person. It's not a crime." I kick a rotted, mushroom-riddled stump out of my path. "Doesn't mean you and I can't come to terms. But first you have to keep us from turning into a smorgasbord for swamp things."

Hoover wags his tail in idiotic glee. Sure, he's cute enough, with his white fur, big black splotches, and droopy ears. And then there are the eyes— huge chocolate pools of innocence that belie his true nature.

I just don't get dogs.

I mean, I know why people like dogs: they are loyal, loving, great companions. The same can be said for Jake. Why would I need a dog when I have him? But Hoover is part of the package. So to show Jake how committed I am to our future, I took Hoover for a bonding walk through the woods.

I sigh as the hound loops us around another dead end ripe with the smell of decayed leaves. Cypress knees and needle palms poke at us with every turn and I half expect to find Yoda around the next bend. If only!

"Come on, mutt. Pick a direction and try for a straight line." If Jake were here, he'd probably laugh and say Hoover was hunting the juiciest toad.

He'd better not be.

Hoover had better be using one hundred percent of that two-ounce brain wrapped in fifty pounds of beagle bacon to get us back to camp.

Resembling a blimp with short legs, he sniffs his way, I hope, one step closer to Jake.

Jake must be frantic. It's been hours. He must have gathered a search party by now. How far lost are we to have not run into anyone? I swat three more mosquitos, praying I don't look like a model for a calamine lotion commercial. I itch all over and sweat stings the scrapes as it rolls down my body. What I wouldn't give for a spa treatment and a tall glass of heaven.

To my right, something snaps in the brush and scurries, as a bigger something plops and splashes to my left. I stifle a scream and stop. Hoover's tail brushes my legs as I pull the leash tighter.

Great thing about the Florida woods is, not only are there bears to worry about, there are also gators to stumble across. Hoover gives me a soulful look and whines.

"I know, boy." I squat beside him. "I'm scared too."

He puts his head on my knee and I give him a reassuring squeeze. "You get us out of here and you and I will have a date with a giant juicy steak."

The word steak does the trick. With a howl, he gathers his second wind and bounds toward yet another brackish vine-choked corner of hell.

Without any survival skills of my own, I put my remainder of hope in Hoover. Never mind that he's twelve years old and has a bit of a limp, his nose is true. I've never had more faith in any other living being.

With a tug and a happy bark, he lunges toward a clearing.

I knew it! He's found his way! He's led us to Jake!

I run after him, tripping on roots with a smile plastered to my face.

He does a little dance of joy and pulls me right up to . . . a dead squirrel.

"You stupid, worthless, fat-ass mutt! All you think about is your stomach! Why did I trust you?" Dropping the leash, I turn away from Hoover's one course meal and sit in the middle of this God-forsaken paradise. Its mossy smell resembles death. "This is it," I cry, as the damp ground seeps through my shorts. This is where the vines and roots weave over me and the earth swallows me like a memory.

It's my fault too, for being so helpless. I can't blame this dumb dog for my problems. I'm the one who was supposed to lead us. He trusted me to get him back to Jake and I let him down. If we get out of this alive, I swear to quit Pilates and take survival training.

With a whine like an anemic tea kettle, Hoover saunters over and drops the rodent tail at my feet.

I laugh at the disgusting bristles and pet him on the head. "Thanks for sharing."

With a yip, he runs in a circle, looks me in the eye, and takes off.

"Hey, wait!" I run after him, not sure if I'm more worried about being stuck out here alone, or being found without Jake's dog.

Around a stand of tall pines, I find Hoover. He barks happy yaps at Jake.

Jake!

Jake lies in the hammock—exactly where I left him. A dozen crushed beer cans are scattered in a circle below him, like a clock counting the hours we've been gone.

"Oh, hey." He blinks back sleep and gives Hoover an ear scratching. "Have a nice time?"

I blink in return.

I understand now why Jake loves Hoover so much. He's a true friend. He took care of me, kept me company, and got me back safe.

There are two things I know to be true this very moment: I would sooner marry Hoover than marry Jake; and I'm going to miss that mutt.

Laurie Ross

40

The Rattlesnake

"Keep out of the pool until your mother comes home."

"I know, Dad," said Becky as she poured milk into her cereal.

"And all of the important phone numbers are on the fridge."

"I know," she said. "Don't answer the door. Don't leave toys on the floors. Vacuum the living room."

"And ask permission before you borrow part of my uniform for your drawings."

Her father's broad-brimmed campaign hat lay on the kitchen table, covered in pencil shavings and surrounded by a series of sketches in crayon. Becky read the trivia on the back of the cereal box and avoided his glare.

The radio on his hip erupted in a garbled request from dispatch, interrupting the lecture.

"This is Henderson," he said. "Acknowledged." He put the radio back on his belt, grabbed his hat, and put on his sunglasses. The dark aviators shielded his eyes from the Florida sun but also made him look like a stranger. "Right. Your mother should be home by five. Please behave."

It was the vacation between the fourth and fifth grades and the first summer Becky was home alone. After breakfast and morning cartoons it was time for chores. She raced the vacuum across the living room carpet, missing half of the dirt.

The pool may have been off-limits, but there were no rules about the surrounding mulch landscape. She knelt on her beach blanket and used a shovel to expose the lizard remains she buried at the start of summer break. In her eagerness to recover the specimen, most of the bones were crushed, but the skull was still intact. It was thin, like tissue paper.

Becky cradled the skull in her palm and took it inside to the kitchen. With her free hand, she pushed the hat drawings to one end of the breakfast table to make room for a makeshift artist studio. A folded napkin served as a soft cushion for the skull. Her supplies were diverse—sketch pads, colored pencils, charcoal, inks, and watercolor trays.

There was a pile of old educational posters from Florida Fish and Wildlife rolled up under her bed. Becky searched the collection until she found the one she needed—a series of over a dozen reptilian skulls. She darted back to the kitchen and used the salt and pepper shakers to lay the poster flat. The brown anole, *Anolis sagrei*, was joined by other common lizards near the top of the poster.

She decided colored pencils were the best choice. It was important to get the skull's unique shape just right—learning how to change pressure on the pencil for more realism would come later. Her lines were dark, and contrasted with the white paper. Still, her drawing of the lizard resembled the one on the poster and the original on the table.

After sketching the skull from two different angles—a top view and a side view, just like in the guidebooks—it was time to display the skull in the office.

The office windows were south-facing, so the room stayed cool even on the hottest days. In the far corner, award certificates and diplomas flanked a computer hutch, but most of the room served as a small museum. A curio protected the most valued part of the collection—a raccoon skull, a key deer hide, fragments of a fossilized giant sloth, and broken bits of Indian pottery. The walls were covered with bird identification guides and watercolors of flatwoods and hammocks. One bookcase was devoted to an encyclopedia set and more than a decade of *National Geographic* magazines. The second bookcase was crammed with guidebooks and paperbacks on every shelf, save one. That shelf belonged to Becky for her own discoveries.

She pulled an index card from the hutch and wrote *Anole skull, July 24, 1994, Rebecca Henderson* with a purple pen. As an afterthought, she added *Henderson backyard, found dead.* She placed the skull and index card near the other summer discoveries—pressed wildflowers and a discarded snakeskin. There was also a jar of shark teeth from the Peace River and a broken manatee rib from a nearby limestone quarry.

Becky stepped back from her shelf. The backyard was proving a disappointing site.

She studied the cow skull on top of the bookcase. It came from the pasture behind the house. The old rancher that owned the property had offered the skull to the family as an exchange for one of her mother's watercolor paintings.

The pasture would have plenty to discover.

It was shortly after ten o'clock. Her parents rarely came home for lunch, and she didn't want to wait until late afternoon to ask about exploring the pasture. Besides, they had only warned her about the pool; no one had said anything about going beyond the backyard.

Becky found her 110 camera and an empty shoebox. She made sure the back door was unlocked—she didn't want to be stuck on the patio all afternoon if she locked herself outside—and made her way beyond the backyard to the pasture fence. There was a new sign advertising the construction of another subdivision, near the spot where her father climbed over to visit the rancher. It was difficult for someone her height to clear the fence, but after a few attempts she vaulted over.

The sun shone down, unfiltered by cloud cover. It was too early in the day for a summer storm. Turkey vultures surveyed the surrounding landscape from a century-old oak tree. The cattle herd—about nine cows—rested in the shade. They took no interest in Becky's arrival. A pair of nearby Sandhill cranes, however, discreetly moved farther into the pasture. Insects, hidden in the grass, buzzed and occasionally took to the air to evade the screeching blue jays.

About twenty yards from the fence lay the remains of a tree struck by lightning in the previous summer. Becky started at one end of the dead tree and checked the nooks for anything of interest.

She almost missed a fence lizard basking near the opposite end. It was wider and squatter than the anole with rough keeled scales that blended in perfectly with the wood, a muted contrast to the bright blue belly underneath.

Becky took a few pictures before she realized that once she developed the film it would be impossible to find the lizard camouflaged on the trunk. The best thing would be to catch it and take photos of it on the glass patio table. She could even take a picture of the blue scales from underneath the glass before releasing the lizard.

She set the camera and shoebox down before jumping onto the trunk and cupping her hands over the lizard. The lizard slipped through a gap in her fingers, darted off, and disappeared into the grass.

There was no time to feel disappointed. A loud rattle drowned out the noise of the insects and the birds and the distant traffic. She froze, motionless as a rabbit. Keeping as still as possible, she looked down at the ground next to the trunk. Underneath the tall grass was dark earth of dead leaves, broken sticks, and soil. The grass swayed in the breeze, causing all the shadows to dance, but something else shifted with a more deliberate movement. The sun randomly revealed glimpses of scales in dark browns and yellows.

Becky knew the right thing to do was to stay still. But what was she supposed to do after that? The rattle continued. It was difficult to think with the constant drone.

The scales continued to slide unhurried under the grass.

Thirty seconds or thirty minutes passed—it was impossible to tell. Sweat beaded on her face. She wanted to run. But what if the snake bit her? Would she just drop immediately? Could she make it home in time? She just wanted to go home. It didn't even matter what sort of trouble she would be in for wandering into the pasture alone. Anything was better than the rattle and the movement within the shadows.

"Becky," said her father behind her.

His voice was soft and low but she could hear it over the rattle. He was only a few feet away.

"You're doing fine. Just stay still."

The rattle continued.

"He's not cornered," said her father. "He'll leave in his own time. Be patient."

The breeze stopped and she could make out the full size of the snake in the still grass. It was impossible to guess the length because of all the coiling, but it looked about three inches across the widest part.

And then the rattle stopped. The snake straightened out of the contorted arrangement of scales and retreated from the tree trunk.

"Is he gone?" he asked. "Stay there and wait for me."

The static from his radio grew louder as he approached the trunk. Becky kept still, dreading to look up and see her father's face—his sunglasses would not completely mask his disapproval.

She kept her head down as he turned the radio off, lifted her from the trunk, and set her down on the grass.

He knelt and brushed the broken pieces of bark and dirt off her knees and arms. She had never seen his face so colorless. His mouth was slightly open, but instead of finding the right words to say he wiped a smudge of dirt from her cheek and grinned. She smiled back.

They walked back to the house, leaving the pasture to the insects and the jays.

She squeezed his hand, unwilling to let go.

At Riverbend Park

—After "At Riverbend Park" by Ralph Papa

Improbable birds, why have they settled
on the banks of the Loxahatchee to become

sawgrass and cattail for the day? Thatched,
swampy roof, their wings are neither question

nor answer but a landscape of both, partners
to the current dredged by the peacock's careless tail.

This is no serenity spell. Under them, the blood
from Seminole battles continues to run, the soil more

magenta than the feathers of the roseate spoonbill.
The sandhill crane is a barren citrus tree; the flocks

of parrots behead the palms when they lift away,
leaving only the echoes of their complaints behind.

Terrie Dahl Thomas

46

PAR

That was the name of our dog. Tante Timise baptized him so. After all, it was her dog in the end.

I will not wait until the end of the story to tell you what PAR stood for: PAR stood for parasite. That's what it stood for, with good reason.

PAR wandered off the main road and into Aunt Timise's yard on a warm, sunny spring morning after she had opened her summer kitchen for the first time. This summer kitchen had been the winter woodshed alongside the house. From then until fall, that's where all the meals would be cooked and eaten. She had the place swept clean and the old wood stove ready to cook. The other meager furnishings, consisting of some chipped, rickety, red-painted chairs and a round table, were as ready as they would ever be for her summer guests.

The kitchen door was opened for light and ventilation. It was only closed at night after a full day of activities, or when rain, carried by the wind, would dampen the modest interior.

One day, Tante Timise was on her way to the well to get her average two pails of water for the day's washing and cooking. As she came out of the kitchen door, she noticed a dog making his way toward her, his tail wagging, his pace steady. She stopped to watch this unwelcome guest. Just as if it was his home, and acting with all the effrontery possible, the dog walked past Tante Timise, looked around, then jumped on her cushioned rocker. Without fear, without a backward glance, he laid himself comfortably down to snooze.

This kind of contempt did not sit well with Timise. Without a word, she approached the chair, grabbed the mutt by the scruff of his neck, put him out in the summer kitchen and, pointing his head toward the road, she gave him an indignant kick in the butt. She grabbed her two galvanized pails and headed for the well. When she returned with her water, PAR was asleep in her rocking chair.

She did not know who owned this nervy animal, but she did not want it. She carried him all the way to the main road and pushed him off. He went some forty feet or so. As she was returning to her kitchen, she looked back. PAR was on her heels. She stopped and stared at him. PAR stopped and stared back and barked once. Tante Timise made a growling sound. PAR was puzzled. Bobbing his head from side to side, he stared, wondering what this growling meant. Timise smiled. PAR had a home.

All PAR ever did was eat and sleep, but he followed Timise wherever she went. He followed her to church, and the first time he even followed her up to the pew. She had to tie him outside. He did not growl nor bark at being tied up. He jutted his front paws straight out, rested his head on them, and went to sleep until mass was over.

I tried playing games with him. I would throw a stick for him to fetch; he got it back once. I tried it again with my new red sponge ball, with no better results. He would not play. He was the laziest dog I ever saw.

PAR never chased or bothered with the animals of the farm. Tante Timise tried to train him to chase the chickens from the veranda. No way. If he saw an animal asleep, he'd go over and keep it company. He would not chase another dog or any other stray animal that came to the house. Cats sneered at him for his indifference. He was the raccoon's best friend. The only time he showed energy was when he was served food.

Timise said he only barked once. I took her word for it. I never heard him bark or even growl. All I ever saw him do was eat and sleep. However, if Tante Timise went anywhere, he ran behind her on his short little legs with his pendulous ears hanging loose. If she stopped and sat down, he'd lie down and sleep.

On a farm, to be of value, you have to earn your keep. For a dog, some of his duties would be to guard the property, to help gather the cows at milking time and chase feral or marauding animals. PAR did none of this. Timise finally gave up on him and called him a parasite. She kept him, however, not with pride, but out of pity.

One day following her regular routine of washing the breakfast dishes, sweeping the kitchen and fetching her daily two pails of water, she lit the old wood stove. She wanted the oven hot to bake some pies. It was a treat she baked for my brother and me when we spent the weekend with her. She then decided to go to her garden and do some weeding and cultivating until the oven got ready for her baking.

The parasite mutt, who had been sleeping with one eye open, watched her every move. When she grabbed her straw hat, and placed it on her head, he knew she was going somewhere. He followed her, as usual. In the garden, he found the shade of a big, bushy tomato plant. He lay on the cool ground and went to sleep.

ODET

Tante Timise worked away. She would throw bunches of weeds over PAR's head outside the garden. Every hail of weeds would disturb PAR's sleep, but he would doze between the disturbances. When the weeding was done in that area, she moved to the far end of the garden to cultivate and weed the rows of potatoes, her most important crop. Suddenly she heard PAR barking. She was surprised, to say the least, by the sudden display of life on the part of her dog. She turned to look at him. He had departed toward the kitchen, running like mad and barking his head off. She started after him to investigate this unusual behavior of PAR. She had not gotten far when she noticed smoke coming out of the kitchen door. As she entered, she saw the floor aflame in front of the stove. Quickly, she poured her pails of water over the flame and doused the fire. She ran back to the well and, returning to the fire, she poured more water over the smoldering planks. After she was sure that the fire was completely out, she proceeded to clean up the mess.

She pulled her big rocking chair out of the kitchen, stacked the other chairs on the table and, with a mop made from old rags, she soaked the water off the floor. It was a mess, and it took her a lot of time and effort to clean up. Exhausted by the excitement and the work, she decided to sit outside in her rocker to rest a bit. When she went out, she found PAR sound asleep in the rocking chair as if nothing had happened. She did not disturb him this time.

After this incident, she made every effort to change PAR's name to something more suitable. It did not matter to him. PAR answered to PAR and did not give a hoot about the name. All he wanted was his lunch and his sleep.

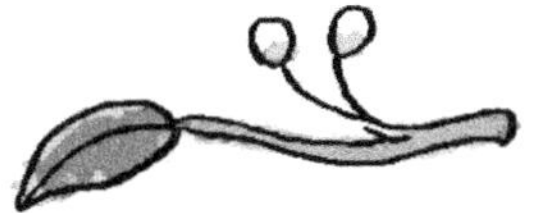

1967

We were three bored Yankee girls
that June, escaping our world
as far south as the red
Camaro would take us,
which was Clearwater, Florida,
in time to watch the sunrise.

Trading dull clerical jobs
for bikinis, sandals, mini-skirts,
we'd left our boyfriends,
dreary parents' lives, and
the grey smog of Northwest Indiana.

The radio blared psychedelic tunes,
as we cruised Gulf roads,
high on beaches, bougainvillea,
and tanned Southern guys
with seductive coastal accents—
free love an invitation
and a curse we misconstrued.

Hendrix sang "Are You Experienced?"
Well, we weren't.

The Cove

We loved the inky rainbows that lapped up against the seawall. On this particular stretch of the bay, only a few boats remained at the docks and the remainder of our little cove was reserved for a condo or two and a pricey surf and turf joint. Just past the restaurant's valet stand, across the small parking lot, stood the low-slung, moss colored hotel our dad called home. His precise address varied from time to time but his main residence was room 147. Like most of the rooms around the edge of the property, his modest territory opened directly onto a breezeway, avoiding the musty hallways reserved for the more traditional, interior spaces. By default, the not so grand parking lot was our front yard most weekends and holidays. The room itself was simple: a bed, a small table, accompanying chairs, and a modest kitchenette. The saving grace of the space was that its rear wall was a series of sliding glass doors that provided access to a tiny balcony, a view of the pool and a bit further, the bay.

Florida has an abundance of a welcoming sort of magic. Perhaps it's a lasting legacy of the state's early explorer and adventurer days. There exists a tacit acknowledgment that if you can make it here, manage the heat, ignore the mosquitos and praise the sunsets, you're welcome to stay and escape the cold realities of the north. Of course, there are exceptions to this mindset, but sincere or not, the come-as-you-are culture of Southwest Florida draws an eclectic and entrepreneurial sort. My grandparents migrated here in the '60s for the sole purpose of catching tarpon and wearing trendy, tropical prints year-round. Long after the initial days of leisure and fishing ended, my father made the decision to raise us here in their complicated version of the laid-back Florida lifestyle. The end result was two sun-kissed kids occupying a place made for people with too much time allotted to drinking and fishing.

Most mornings at the hotel my sister Anne and I were eager to play and explore. We'd skip down the concrete stairs barefoot and make our way over to the restaurant, treading lightly along yellow parking lines in order to save the scorched bottoms of our feet. We'd sneak to the rear of the building, just along the water, and create our own ad hoc fishing village. Poles in hand, Anne and I would search for something to make the endless sitting more comfortable: an old cushion that had dislodged itself from a sun lounger, a broken milk crate, a stray phone book, or even a Styrofoam cooler purchased in haste by the tourist who had no intention of packing it up and carting it back to Cleveland. Fortunately, there was an abundance of related flotsam and jetsam on which we could rest our tiny bodies and try to fish. We'd get ourselves situated, sometimes with a few pieces of white bread between us, snacking on some and making bait with the rest. God help the miserable creatures who hooked themselves onto our lines for a tiny taste of wet Wonder Bread.

At other times, we'd abandon the poles and simply scout out the landscape, taking care not to fall into the dark and murky drink. Who knows what the restaurant let loose in the water behind the kitchen, but it seemed to attract a wide variety of half-dead fish, determined to navigate the shallow depths for a crumb or two of last night's special. If the parking lot acted as our front yard, these sad fish could count as our almost pets.

Eventually, we'd run out of bread and patience. Morning would creep into lunchtime and we'd begin the process of figuring out our next move. With little to no money, few staples in the mini fridge and even less oversight or parenting, our options were limited.

"Let's just check in with Dad," we'd suggest to each other with only meager amounts of hope. "Maybe he has a plan."

After gathering the poles, we'd trace our steps back toward room 147. Despite the years of weekends at the hotel, I have no memory of ever finding the door locked. We'd come and go as we pleased, no key or special precautions needed. I'm not sure if this was a sign of a lack of care or a lack of valuables on the other side of the door. Anne and I would travel the grounds so effortlessly. It was an ease that did little to betray the true complexity of two curious young kids roaming the sometimes-shabby property alone.

We swung the door open and it was easy to quickly scan the entire room and see that our dad wasn't there. "Wanna make something to eat?"

"Not really. We ate all of the crackers yesterday with the last of the butter and jelly."

"Maybe there's something else. Hmmm, sardines, some leftover carry-out, an orange . . ."

"Let's just go get a hot dog. Dad's probably at the Chickee."

Chickees are a backcountry-style structures once used by the Seminole tribes and still used by some Miccosukee villages. Our fair city's proximity to the Everglades allowed for some architectural overflow of the indigenous dwellings to inform local resort culture. Thatch on the top, open at the sides, it was practical to locals and exotic to tourists. For our purposes, Chickee meant bar; the hotel watering hole and social center of the pool and marina areas. This was our part-time home and as long as we stayed out of obvious trouble, we came and went as we pleased.

The open-air bar was tended to by Alex, a regal, white-haired gentleman who spoke with an impossibly thick Scottish accent. His stakeholders were the hotel management, the regulars in various states of sobriety, and the seasonal snow-bird tourists. To him, Anne and I were akin to stray cats. He was hesitant to feed us for fear we'd keep returning and he'd have to tend to us in greater detail. For the most part, we developed an unspoken agreement; if we stayed somewhat invisible, he'd turn a blind eye to the fact that we had become regulars at the bar, accepting hot dogs and maraschino cherries as fine feasts on days when little else was available.

As time went on, Alex grew to appreciate our situation. He occasionally commented on our impeccable manners and would even toss a compliment or two in our direction when a tourist's kid grew emboldened and tried to take a seat at the bar. The unspoken rule was that you could reach up between the anchor shaped ashtrays, just beyond the rum punches to collect your handouts, but were expected to quickly transition to the perimeter of the bar. Certainly, no one wanted to sidle up next to flip-flopped kids when they planned on doing some serious day drinking.

Breezing past the regulars, most of which we knew by their first names, their nicknames or their boats' names, we spotted our dad smiling and holding court.

"Hey, Dad, we're hungry. Came to get a hot dog."

"Sure, just talk to Alex. And take it to a table."

"We know, just checking in. We'll eat and then go back upstairs after. Maybe swimming later. Just letting you know."

The beauty of the exchange is that he didn't ask us about our plans. He had complete trust in the ability of two young children to feed, water, and care for themselves. At the bar, he was always in good company. Whatever their reasons, folks came to the Chickee to drink and share their mostly embellished or wholly untrue stories. As expected, talk consisted of fishing trips, fortunes up north, possible younger wives, and imagined financial trades. My dad made friends quickly and his natural charm, his innate ability to garner goodwill from others, regardless of his life's choices, was extraordinary. Occasionally, when we couldn't overhear details of the more outrageous stories, he'd do his own editing and fill us in on the most interesting tidbits. He'd regale us with tales of friends headed off to Cuba or Spain, or of new boats procured by dubious means. We'd listen, attending to every word as if these were state secrets being passed between a chosen few.

Eating our hot dogs a few paces away from Dad's barstool, Anne and I marveled at how lucky we were not to have boring old Saturdays like our friends at school. We would sit and look out beyond the bay at the sun setting on the flotilla of yachts, boats, and dinghies. Our feet would cautiously skim the surface of the water from the seawall as we said very little.

By all accounts, the natural parts of Florida are breathtakingly beautiful. The bay's calm waters perfectly reflect the intensity of the sky in a way that is impossible to replicate on film or by memory. During the best of evenings, the air was full, slightly damp, and almost cool to the touch making it impossible to deny the tropical DNA of the place.

In the same way that friends pine away for the feel of crisp fall air of their northeast childhoods, I'm nostalgic for the feel of salt and sea on my skin after a long day outside. The sights and smells of a Florida childhood are ripe with opportunity and life. For Anne and I, the distinct aroma of boat diesel, of suntan lotion, of Cutty Sark, and of raw coconut meld together to create a specific schema.

Marcia Morley

Inverness

By the time we moved to Florida,
and thought to search for relatives,
my Aunt Madelyn had already died,
having retired to Citrus County
long before I knew she'd left Chicago.

I picture her on Main Street,
in the blue shuttered book store,
sun-bronzed refugee from northern winters,
sandals skipping the clock tower square
in mid-November.

Perhaps she stayed that first year
at the Crown, its century-old facade
regal as a white-laced queen,
wide porches catching breezes
from the Withlacoochee.

Now, past the river, past the shops
with rock 'n roll posters, memorabilia,
we lose ourselves on winding streets,
eventually finding the courthouse where,
facing the bench, a cutout Elvis stands
witnessing trials since 1961
when *Follow That Dream* was filmed here.

Today we still see him everywhere.

Around the corner, Coach's has burgers
and Cuban sandwiches, ubiquitous in this state,
baseball on flat screen and craft beer signs—
one of a handful of places
escaped from the 60s—also where
The King is not in the building.

I want to time travel to 1961,
sit on a porch swing listening to
Love Me Tender on the radio,
hug my aunt one last time,
maybe ask her
if she'd seen Elvis.

Magical Florida

My first eight years were spent in Tampa so my earliest memories are of sunshine and palm trees. My father was stationed at MacDill and, like many military families, we built a life here. My mother worked at Maas Brothers, now long gone. My older sister and I went to school at Christ the King and the Academy of the Holy Names. On weekends, my family, Irish-American, fish-belly pale, would drive over to St. Pete Beach for a day in the sun that would leave us all red, blistered and cranky. My father was transferred overseas when I was eight so we packed up and moved leaving Florida behind, at least for a few years.

My second sojourn in the area came several years later, in 1959. In these intervening years our family had imploded, torn apart by forces it would take me years to understand. My mother and I fled to Tampa, a place we knew, eager to escape bad memories and bleak winters. We lived in what is now called "Old Seminole Heights" but which back then was just another Tampa neighborhood. I walked to Memorial Junior High where the kids made fun of my Yankee accent and pasty complexion.

In 1961 my mother and I rejoined my father in a doomed attempt to save the family. We moved to Massachusetts where my life unfolded: high school, college, the wild '60s and '70s, a career in IT, two marriages, one bad, one good.

But Florida was not done with me—not yet, anyway. My third and final sojourn in the area began in 2012. This time it was my husband and me, both my parents now long gone, my sister in far-away upstate New York. Seeking relief from New England winters, we decided to move to Florida, and picked the Gulf side of the state. We came down in May, and starting in Venice, we drove north until we found a place we liked, somewhere we wanted to live, even if that meant driving all the way up to the panhandle. But it didn't take that long. We drove over the Sand Key Bridge and fell in love. We returned to New Hampshire, sold our condo, and moved to Clearwater in August of that year. Our friends thought we were crazy and maybe we were.

Some of the Florida I remember remains: the Thunderbird Motel on Gulf Boulevard on the way to St. Pete looks like it did then. Driving across the Courtney Campbell Causeway with Tampa Bay on both sides still feels the same. Bay Shore is as beautiful as I remember. We recently located the house my mother and I lived in. It is still there and looks much the same, though, like most memories of the houses in our past, it is smaller and shabbier than I remember.

While some of what I remember remains, but other places from my past are gone: the drive-in theater on Dale Mabry where watched movies, the sound coming from speakers hooked on the car window, my sister and I falling asleep in the back seat. Webb's City-The World's Most Unusual Drugstore, where we stopped whenever we drove to St. Pete. The Zi-Chex Restaurant on Gandy Boulevard where we met my father on his return from the Korean War. I cried uncontrollably because I didn't recognize him in his fatigues and with a newly-grown beard.

I am still fish-belly pale, a transplanted New Englander, once again enjoying the blue skies, white egrets and swooping pelicans, flowers in February, and the turquoise water of the Gulf. I love it all—the outdoor craft shows year 'round, farmers' markets brimming with local produce, white beaches, glimpses of dolphins arching out of the water, Third Fridays in Safety Harbor, Greek fishermen in Tarpon Springs. I love it that I don't need to put on boots, mittens, a hat, scarf and puffy winter coat just to walk out the door.

That I am here again 50+ years later, at this stage in my life, baffles, surprises, and delights me. Life is more mysterious and magical than I ever imagined.

The Belle's View

The Lady on the hill stood waiting,
catching salt mist from the bay that made
her heart of pine exterior glisten
when the sun descended.
The Southern Belle was arranged
in the Victorian way.
She looked out over the long pier, scrub pines,
mangroves, and palms.
Gulls and egrets chatted it up,
anticipating the train that delivered visitors,
who came to relax
and luxuriate in this place of swamps.

The Ladies who came wore long dresses
of layered gauze
and button-up ostrich leather boots,
too much for the heat
but as little as propriety would allow—
their hats adorned with exotic plumes.
The egrets and spoonbills took offense.
Rich, powerful men
crowded the platform,
while coach attendants helped families
into high-wheeled carriages
that would jostle them up the hill
on a road of crushed shells.
The carriages brought inventors,
investors, industrialists, and royalty.
Their trunks were loaded on rail stock
Moved along on tracks that transferred them
via tunnels running beneath

richly carpeted floors
and her magnificent entrance.
A cool marble lobby
offered the first glimpse
of her Queen Anne architecture.

The Belle had 145 rooms.
Her guests were fed and pampered
after the grime of travel
was washed away in porcelain bowls
filled with scented water,
freshly drawn.
Ever the elegant
and gracious hostess—
discrete and beautiful,
Privy to secrets whispered
within her walls.

There were parlor games,
tennis on the lawn, bicycle races,
yachting, fishing, and billiards.
There were affairs of a carnal nature,
and those of white linen toppers
set with fine china and cut crystal—
in the dining room or at the pool,
with compliments to the Chef.

In the ball room
the sun imposed itself
through Tiffany windows,
not intimidated by their fame.
Together they collaborated

to create prisms on the walls,
the guests,
and the occasional paper-white, linen gown.
The house orchestra played.

It was a scandal
when young Morton Plant fell in love,
paying Maisie's husband generously
to go away.
They wed, but her demands were great.
She coveted Cartier pearls and he would not buy them,
so she traded their Townhouse for them.
Cartier moved in.

"The White Queen of the Gulf,"
as the Belle's admirers called her,
opened for business in 1897.
She withstood searing heat and brutal storms.
The Depression did not spare her.
The gulf became menacing,
a possible passage for enemy submarines.
Elegance gave way to utility,
providing beds for the soldiers of World War Two.

The Belle remained on the hill
and glistened in many more sunsets
long after the train and trestle were gone.
Still, dignitaries came—
presidents, past and future,
characters of note.
They were a more casual breed,
those mid- twentieth century souls.

Dylan stayed in a cottage
where he painted, with great abandon,
on canvases propped against antique chairs.
He upended cigarette butts and
set them in lines across the table,
like little picket fences.
Joan was there too.
They built a bonfire on the golf course.
They were the defiant young.

The White Queen fell to disrepair,
but still people came
and *still* they were accommodated,
though within a more tired elegance.
She hosted conventions of hairdressers,
Primitive Baptists, realtors, art exhibits,
ballroom dance competitions,
and the occasional class reunion.
All were welcome.
Purple wine stained the carpet
that lay over floors warped from humidity.
Ceiling plaster fell
and mold grew between the baseboards.

Her structure, now sagging and tired—
like so many "ladies of a certain age."
a bone of contention
between developers
and resolute supporters.
Commissioners and businessmen,
decided that she, an historical landmark,
was not worth the money
commonly spent on stadiums.
Besides, they said,
who wants to stay in a place where you can't walk to the beach?

The Belle came down over the tunnels,
bringing with her
the Duke of Windsor's favorite rooms,
and the ghosts of the fourth floor.
The hallways where Edison, Ford,
and the Vanderbilts walked
piled high with broken heart of pine.
No more parties or secrets
or lunches on the terrace.
No more prisms on the wall.

She was just a building
        after all.

Terrie Dahl Thomas

Walt Belcher

Memories of Trains Gone By

A train whistle in the night is a forlorn sound. It's a haunting wail that cuts through the silence and serves as a melancholy reminder of a bygone era, recalling a time in America when trains carried more than freight, a time when the rails linked towns, large and small.

For more than a century locomotives were taking people away or bringing people home, opening a new chapter in life, or closing another. In the 1800s those "Iron Horses" became part of the folklore of the old West, inspiring novels and movies well into the 20th Century.

A train whistle fading in the distance came to symbolize the heartbreak of lost love, inspiring country music songs like Hank Williams' "I'm So Lonesome I Could Die."

Hear that lonesome whippoorwill, He sounds too blue to fly. The midnight train is whining low. I'm so lonesome I could cry.

I think of that song and others when I hear the CSX freighters roll through Safety Harbor, cutting across Main Street a few times each day. Even as I write this, one is rambling by. I live close enough to hear the rumble of the cars rolling on the rails.

Our nation's romance with trains peaked in the 1940s, before my time, and faded in the 1950s when I was a little kid. But I know about that romance from old movies, old songs and old stories. Train songs also are part of my musical heritage from Jimmie Rodgers' "Train Whistle Blues" to Johnny Cash singing "The Orange Blossom Special." I can even recite the lyrics to Willie Nelson's "Railroad Lady." The train cuts across all musical genres. "The Chattanooga Choo-Choo" was a hit for Glenn Miller's big band in the '40s. The Monkees took "The Last Train to Clarksville" in the '60s. And folk singer Arlo Guthrie had a hit with "City of New Orleans" in the '70s.

A train whistle has never disturbed my sleep. I have heard it at 3 a.m. when I couldn't sleep anyway. And it's always been a sweet sound, one that carries me back to childhood.

I grew up in Greenville, South Carolina, where freight trains crisscrossed the numerous textile mill communities on the southwest side of town. Freight trains, loaded with textile goods, bustled in and out of the mills almost daily. Our community was called City View, but there was no view of any city, just a textile mill and rows of small clapboard mill houses. We were on the wrong side of the tracks as far as social and economic status was concerned.

Passenger service had just about died out by the time I was in elementary school. Greenville's train station had become a shabby, lonely place. The Greyhound bus station saw more action.

But every morning there was a line of box cars outside Southern Weaving Company and Woodside Mill, the two textile plants that were on my paper route. At one point, these cars blocked my path to easy delivery. Instead of walking down the tracks to the front of the line, I would climb over the couplings between two box cars and be on my way. If that train had ever started moving, I might have been cut in half or lost a leg. But I figured that the cars wouldn't be going anywhere until the mill's first shift which began at 7 a.m.

Was that dangerous? Yes. And so was been putting pennies on the tracks to watch them get smashed flat by a passing train. But I was 12 then and more lucky than smart.

In the late 1960s at the University of Georgia, I was introduced to the so-called "track people" and their rowdy Saturday football parties. This hardy band of fans would scale a wooden railway trestle that skirted the west end of Sanford Stadium. They got a free viewing of the Georgia Bulldogs' gridiron action. And, unlike the 50,000 paying fans in the stadium, they could openly imbibe alcoholic beverages. During afternoon games, the train whistle here took on a whole new meaning. It sent the "track people" scampering for safety. After the train crept by, they would scramble back up the trestle. I think the engineer gave an extra "Go Dawgs!" toot. This tradition started in the 1930s and continued until the early 1980s when the stadium added more seats, blocking the trestle view.

My first train ride wasn't until the 1980s when I wrote a travel article for *The Tampa Tribune* about taking short day trips on a part of the Amtrak line that runs between Tampa and Winter Park. There were stops in Lakeland and Plant City. It's not the most scenic of routes—kudzu, industrial wastelands and neighborhoods that have seen better days. Tampa's Union Station, which had been a magnificent example of Italian Renaissance architecture when it opened in 1912, was falling apart. It has since been restored and is now a historic landmark.

Today, those unfamiliar with the notion of a plaintive "whistle" in the night may consider it an annoying horn, especially if it wakes them up at 3 a.m. In some Florida cities, ear-sensitive residents have battled city and railroad officials in an effort to silence the train whistles. By law, a train in Florida must sound a warning for at least 15 seconds as it approaches a road. Those four toots—two long, one short and one long—have about the same decibel level as a chain saw; but people living close to the tracks says that's too much. I say the tracks were there first. If you build an abode close enough for a train whistle to give you a headache, then get ear plugs. That whistle lasts only a few seconds. And it carries a lot of history when it blows. In Safety Harbor, it is part of the local culture. Patrons of the Whistle Stop Grill and Bar play a drinking game when the CSX rolls by and sounds its horn. I've only traveled on American trains a couple of times since that 1982 excursion. And I had not paid attention to a train whistle in years—not until I moved to Safety Harbor. Now when I hear that whistle, I smile and think of all the times that trains passed through my life. And I'm not on the wrong side of the tracks anymore.

I Am the Voice

I've been described
as the voice of Maya Angelo
in Safety Harbor.
Oh so flattering, but so inaccurate,
for my body of work is but a cupful
in the vast ocean of Mother Maya's words.

But yes,
I am the voice.

I am the voice of diversity within unity.
You pretend not to see our differences,
for you are good hearted.
But I say *see,* our differences . . .
Celebrate and rejoice
in the glorious variety of God's creation.

I am the voice of the multi-hued face of God
Created in the Image of God.

I am the voice of inclusion
Young, old, yellow, brown, white,
gay, lesbian, straight,
Muslim, Jew, Christian.
For me there are no outcasts . . .
All are dear to my heart.

I am the voice of the beloved and the forsaken
Created in the Image of God.

I am the voice of reason
Like conservatives, I honor and take pride
in the values that shaped our nation.
Except when they exclude or destroy.
Like liberals, I honor change
that enhances the present and repairs the past.
Except when brash and arrogant.

> I am the voice of balance and harmony,
> Created in the Image of God.

I am the voice of enlightened progress
drawing from the wisdom of our elders
joined with the wisdom of our youth.
Together, they create a future
worth passing on to our children.

> I am the voice of our future
> Created in the image of God.

I am the voice of praise,
rejoicing in the community of Safety Harbor.
Embracing its diversity . . . its inclusiveness . . .
its balance and harmony.
Its wisdom, enlightenment and creativity.

> I am but one of Safety Harbor's many voices
> Created in the image of God.

Sun Worn

To escape the suffocating white of her cubicle she'd read
27 novels
12 collections of poetry
13 plays
16 short stories
She was a hermit
Beyond pages of books
Her life was her cubicle
Her cats
Her increasing number of grey hairs
She awoke to the sun
She was surrounded by condos like
Wild island men battling palm trees and lizards
Today she was lucky
She'd walked south
Caught flounder, grouper
Picked oranges, grapefruit, mangos
Papaya and starfruit
When she fell asleep
She dreamt of flying fish
She was greasy curls and sun-worn colored eyes
"Are you alright?" she was asked
She'd been hurling through space
Through time
Through sunshine
"I'm fine," she'd say
"Just reading."

Dianne Persall

The Race

It's a little before 6 a.m. on a Tuesday, and I'm just finishing a three-minute run. I'm glad to be walking for 90 seconds, panting a little on my second mile of the day. I can't run a mile straight, but running with walking breaks I do okay. At this hour, along Bayshore, there are clumps of other early morning runners, some illuminated by reflective gear or glowing cell phone screens, one man with an annoying blinking hat with a blinding white light attached, who is shuffle-running the opposite way. The only people up are runners and dog walkers. In about 20 minutes, when the sun is up a little more and you can start to see the chairs on the docks instead of just the black outline of private docks against the night water, we will see a bicycle or two, racing along, sometimes ringing a bell, sometimes just passing with a jangle of gears and whoosh of air as they speed by.

I've been listening to my favorite wake up and run tracks on my wireless headphones, but I'm almost out of juice. Now I have to just 'imagine' my favorite songs, but I've been doing this route and listening to this particular mix for a couple of years now. I'm passed by a man and his sheepdog, no leash, but they're here every morning. The dog has eyes only for the tennis ball the man throws for him to chase and retrieve, chase and retrieve. I decide to power walk past the marina, listening to the sound of the moored boats clinking and clanking to themselves, that sound like wind through bamboo, the sound of boats sitting on the water, settling in. My headphones still have enough juice for the fitness app to say, in a chirpy female voice. "Ready to start the fifth interval. Three . . . two . . . one . . . go." I inhale, puff out a couple times to get my breathing back on track, and get back to a slow jog, running past the boats, past the public restrooms, and head for the Safety Harbor pier.

The pier, like the rest of the town, is sleepy at this time of day. There's a beat-up Toyota Corolla with a weathered paint job, and a heavy-set man in a fishing hat and shorts is there with the trunk open, large bucket at his feet, two fishing rods leaning on the right fender, untangling his fishing net. As I continue my jog, I run down the pier, noticing spatters of bait at several places, and spider webs still intact from the night before. I run down to the end, and there are two women there, like sunrise sentinels, one looking to the south, and a younger one seated on the opposite end looking north. The younger one is squinting at her cell phone, tapping away and the older one is looking out over the water. Since they're both absorbed I don't wave or say hi, not even the perfunctory 'athlete's greeting' we use to acknowledge someone else crazy enough to be up this early working out in the heat, a quick flap of the hand and if either party is feeling particularly jaunty, a quick head bob.

I finish my loop and jog back past the boats in the Marina. As I approach Bayshore I see three girls go by, two younger ones in matching Best Damn Race shirts and behind them, putting on speed to pass, the girl in the red shorts. Dammit. As soon as I see her I begin to jog a little faster, even though my legs are aching. I thought I was here before her! I thought I was first today! She is already sweating and red in the face, obviously she's been running for a while this morning. How many miles? I wonder. Three? Two? Five? There's no way she's done five. There's no way. I pick up my pace, wishing I had my music to help. I run a little faster still, now really panting, and close the distance, I'm now ten yards behind, now five, now three. Close enough to pass if she slows down at all. She hangs a right at the Safety Harbor Spa. She slows her pace a bit on the narrow sidewalk, and I'm able to pass her on the small foot bridge. I hear her breathing hard as I run past her, tired but not giving up. Today, this is mine, today is my day. And, just like that, just as I'm happy to be out front, she passes me and cuts into the neighborhood streets. I am on her heels, a few feet behind, still panting, not giving up.

She loops back again, now heading back toward the large parking lot we both use. I let her run a little bit ahead, then, as she rounds the last corner toward her car, I sprint like a mad woman, giving it all I have, running past her, to touch my car's fender first. Her car is parked next to mine.

She slaps her own fender, signaling she's done. I am bent over, elbows out, hands on my hips, catching my breath. "You know," she says between breaths, "you don't have to chase me. We can run together, Janine."

I grin at her. "What's the fun of that? So, how many miles today?"

"Three and a half. You?

"Two and a half. See you Thursday?"

She sips her water bottle. "See you Thursday."

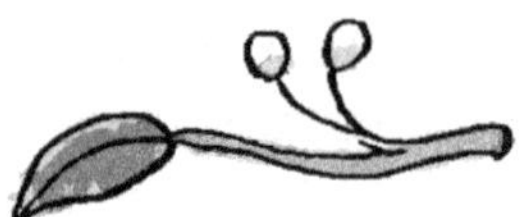

Threads

We were moving my grandmother into a home. Sorting her life into black Sharpie labels and deciding which memories to keep and which to throw away. I hated change.

"Grandma, all of these purses are going, right?" A tangle of leather straps and gold buckles spilled out of a cardboard box.

"Of course, sweetie. A woman needs lots of options."

I knelt down to untangle her options, while she carefully looked on.

"Wait, Beth. What's that? The green one," she said, pointing to an alligator skin purse half-buried in the mess.

"This one?" I grabbed its cucumber finish and handed it up to her.

"Oh heavens, I forgot I had this. It's from Saks. The original one, in New York. Must be fifty years old." She stroked its waxy cheeks gently. "Your grandfather brought it back for me. That was the trip he accidentally took my manicure kit instead of his toiletries," she shook her head. "Always doing stuff like that. This was his apology." She handed it back to me, which was always her way of suggesting something. "Do you want it?"

Instinctively, I opened its metal snap jaws and revealed its mouth, lined with a pomegranate satin. My grandmother had a habit of leaving loose bills in all of her purses, and as a child such scavenging financed many a baseball card from down the street. This one had already been cleaned out, likely by me, years before.

"Thanks, Grandma," I replied, handing it back to her. "But why don't you keep it for now."

"I bet you can't get a pocketbook like this in that city now. Everything's changed." She looked it over once more before passing it back into the box.

I closed up the cardboard canopy and labeled it "KEEP," which had begun as my shorthand for "keepsakes" until Uncle Doug misunderstood it as simply one of two possible categories—"keep" and "trash." Now these two words organized the sum of my grandmother's life.

"It's all part of life, Mom. You know that," Uncle Alan projected from the foyer, amid the stacks of boxes.

"Was that the trip to New York where Dad met Frank Sinatra on the subway?" Uncle Doug said, to no one in particular.

"Frank Sinatra wouldn't take the subway, Doug."

"You don't know whether he did or not. It's possible." Uncle Doug punctuated his last sentence by taping off a box labeled "TRASH."

"Yeah, possible," Uncle Alan said. "Like the deer Dad saw running through downtown. Or the Cuba story."

I shuttled the purses to the foyer, where there were far more "TRASH" labels than I liked. I didn't understand why we had to box up trash, but I guess we just had to box up everything.

"That's my favorite memory of him, you know," Uncle Doug chimed in loudly. "The Cuba story. Just like him."

"You weren't even born yet," Uncle Alan replied.

"I mean of him telling the story. He did go down there, you know. When Castro was trying to take over. He knew things were going to get bad and he wanted to get the company out of there as fast as possible."

"If anyone knew what was going on down there, Doug, it was Uncle Manny, not Dad. He was working with the people, the tabaqueros, closest to the action." Uncle Alan was busy stacking. "Plus Dad didn't speak a lick of Spanish."

"That's why he took Uncle Manny with him down there. They both had interests in Cuba. Almost everyone in Florida did. But Dad always knew what was best for the company."

"Yeah, always," Uncle Alan said under his breath.

"The two of them liquidated the whole company, you know. Every single truck. No more Lawson Truck Sales in Cuba. He had to ride around making all those deals, too. Once on a horse! All just days before the Revolution. Amazing."

"Almost unbelievable."

I returned to the nearby family room. "What about these things by the fireplace, Grandma?" A lone cardboard box sat on the rusty brick hearth, and out of its corner, an embroidered strawberry dangled precariously.

"Oh heavens, Beth, make sure you get that handkerchief," Grandma entreated, as I plucked it from the box. The strawberry's stem was too dark, more like the color of collards, and had unraveled a bit. But the speckled tongue of the strawberry's bulb was ripe and unblemished.

"Where was this from?"

"Well, your grandfather brought it back from one of his adventures, but I did the stitching. When we first got married, I couldn't even boil water, so I had to learn all of that woman's work. I ordered a catalogue on sewing and bought the most expensive thread I could find. This was my first project with it. It's monogrammed, too. See?"

I unfolded the linen to find her familiar initials. "It's very pretty, Grandma. I like the color."

"It was called sanguine. And it's real silk," she said, as I traced the delicate letters. "You know, I had a whole spool of that thread in my little sewing kit but one day it was just gone. For the life of me, I couldn't find it. This is the only thing I got to use it for. Felt something terrible about it going to waste."

I handed the linen up to her, and she folded it back up into its creased quarters. "You don't have a hanky, do you?" I shook my head no. "Every woman needs a hanky, sweetie." Then she predictably tried to hand it back to me. "Do you want it?"

I smiled and repeated, "You keep it for now."

She tucked the strawberry back into the box and I etched out "KEEP" once again. I carried it to the foyer, where Uncle Doug was still packing up the "TRASH" boxes.

"Once they had sold everything off, though, they still had to get all the money back, right? That is my favorite part."

"We've heard this story a million times, Doug. We all know how it ends."

Unphased, Uncle Doug continued, "So Dad goes to the bank and gets all American bills. And then he takes all of the bank envelopes filled with money and sews them into the lining of his jacket!" To signify the jacket, he extended his left arm out and patted the imaginary lining with his right. "All that money. Every last bill. To sneak it all back into the country. It's incredible."

"Dad didn't know how to sew to save his life."

"Uncle Manny knew how to sew, I bet. With nine sisters?" Uncle Doug began on yet another box of trash.

"OK, but where does he get the needle and thread? It's not like he would have randomly brought it down with him."

"It's not like Cuba didn't have needles and thread. For big business men like them, I'm sure someone took care of their needs."

Uncle Alan moved to the other side of the foyer. "Hand me that box, will you?"

Uncle Doug ignore the request and continued, "Getting on the plane was the hard part. When they're ready to board, the security says, 'I'm sorry sir, I'm going to have to pat you down.' 'OK, no problem' Dad says. So, he takes off his suit jacket, hangs it on the coat rack, and puts his arms out." Uncle Doug demonstrated this pose from the floor. "They pat him down, he puts his jacket back on, and walks onto the plane. With all of that money!"

"Yeah, simple as that. Everything is as simple as that."

The last box to be moved was in my grandmother's emptied bedroom. That room was also the heaviest with nostalgia. No more pine hope chest at the foot of the bed, my step stool at night when I had bad dreams. No more carved vanity and delicate wrought-iron stool, where I'd gaze into the see-saw mirror and wait to become a woman.

"What all is in this box, Grandma?" I hadn't seen it before, so my uncles must have packed it.

"Just some old things. They were in the back of your grandfather's armoire, so I just kept them. I'm not even sure what all's in there."

The box bulged with its tattered contents: metallic-tinted photos, some of Uncle Manny's old cigar labels, a handful of jaggedly folded news clippings, and an unused notepad stamped with Lawson Truck Sales letterhead. All of it needed to be repacked.

"Grandma, did Grandpa really go to Cuba?"

"Just let your Uncle Doug tell his story, sweetie."

"I know. But Grandpa used to tell it to me, too."

"How do you remember that? You were so young."

"I just want to know if it's true."

"Oh heavens, I don't know. I never could keep track of his comings and goings. Your grandfather just liked to do his own thing."

"But did you notice a lot of cash all of a sudden? I mean, all that money had to go somewhere, right?"

"That would have been for the company, not for us. I don't know what went on with it. He never said and I never asked." One-by-one, I pulled out thick bundles of memories and portioned them out onto the floor.

"Do you think Frank Sinatra ever took the subway?"

"I find that hard to imagine," she smiled. "But you never know what those Yankees will do."

On the edge of the chaotic spiral of the box's contents, I spotted a packet of papers, pinched by a brittle rubber band into faded bowtie. The band broke when I tried to stretch it off, and the bundle of paper fanned dust in the room.

It appeared towards the edge of the mess, its oddly preserved corner peeking out. A crisp bank envelope with clear block letters. "Banco de Cuba." I pinched it out slowly and pressed open its thin, minnowy lips. No money. But at the bottom, there was a single sanguine thread.

"What's that?" My grandmother asked. I handed it up to her.

She peered into it for the weight of a minute and slowly shook her head.

"Will you look at there," she finally said. Then she handed it back to me. "Do you want it?"

"Yes," I nodded and gently slid the memory into my back pocket. As my grandmother left the room, I quietly repacked the last box and labeled it, "KEEP."

The Big Guava

Where phosphate crumbles at the hands of draglines,
defacing the rocks and robbing its heart of pebbles,

falling into the hands of greedy farmers
who begin planting on the same ground they stole from.

Where sticks of fire burn in the sky
before overburdened clouds exhale in rain showers.

Where streets leave us with the aftertaste of Prohibition;
where the smell of liquor sails on quivering tongues

even after the passing of Sunday morning blues.
Where cigars petrify grey skin and wrinkles,

stuttering in the mouths of men
who came from Cuban soil, the soles of their shoes

swallowing fragments of home and mixing with
Tampa's over cultivated fields, diagnosed with asthma.

Viva Ybor

The streets smell of musk and smoked rain
as men sit on porch steps and talk,
holding cigars between their teeth
like children chew bubblegum;
they speak about life back in Cuba,
reminiscing on white sand and no worries.
They laugh at the world, and how funny it gets
when it tries—-and fails—to strip the rest of your being.
The city is burning with freedom,
and the scent of home
lingers in filled kitchens,
cracking like dust with each pastelito.

Ybor City, *Alaina Virgilio*

Balance Sheet

June 27, 2016. Monday. It is four hours across the state from Juno Beach to Clearwater. Driving home. After a couple of hours on the Turnpike, we stop for gas at Yeehaw Junction. Stepping from the car, I hear a metallic thud, and a grunt.

On the island 20 feet over, a man is sprawled on his side, looking our way. "You need help?" I ask. It is not a question. A raised hand his only reply.

Dark-haired, in his late thirties, he must have been positioning his wheel chair at the pump when, losing his balance, the chair collapsed, dropping him to the ground. Grimacing, arms barely holding him up next to the fallen chair, the man has no legs.

He has collected himself when I get there, pulling himself up, righting the chair, leaning on a wheel, ready for another try.

"Let me get that."

Handing me his card, I stick it in the slot, twisting off the gas cap: "Regular? All the way?" He nods twice, leaning forward punching in his PIN.

Grabbing the handle: "You a vet?"

"Yeah, 9th Marines outta Okinawa. Then Iraq," he says, this time nodding down at nothing.

What More Could I Say?

"Thanks for your service?" The lamest of all possible observances, I follow it with others, equally lame; about our Marine son once serving at those same places, and of meeting my wife in the Air Force during Vietnam.

Look. This took all of 10 minutes. But all along I've known life is a balance sheet: we proceed, for better or worse, adding to or subtracting from our credits and debits. Helping a wounded Marine that afternoon barely moved the credit account that rear-echelon types, like me, use to balance our debits to heroes.

Like him.

Palm Trees

I like to climb the ridges hidden beneath
the layer of skin crocheting the base of the tree
while my fingernails scrape the bark off its
cylindrical body in a sweeping motion.

My favorite palm trees are the old, bent
ones with spines so aged they're perched
in the same position for their entire life span,
and I can walk across them in a straight line.

I rest at the very crook of their neck where the palm
fronds are a welcoming shelter to me, curved
over to see the sweat trickling down my nose
and the relaxation in my iris flourishing rapidly.

Pilgrimage

(In Memory of Marjorie Kinnan Rawlings)

It wasn't easy to find you.
All those twisty back roads
through mosquito-ridden scrub,
starting out from that sleepy town,
Micanopy, its Main Street
as quaint as a diorama.

From your home in Cross Creek,
where I lingered longer than I planned,
pondering the immense solitude,
another half-dozen or so miles,
winding through thick woods,
and across a railroad track.

I found the burial ground just in time,
before the sun had sunk behind the trees.
Although I'm sure you'd
have forgiven me if I'd driven straight past.
There's not much there to see.
Just a series of flat stones, and some listing
monuments that resemble unfinished statues.

It's called Antioch — the cemetery —
an ancient name which seems fitting —
out there in Island Grove.
I sought you out among the grander tombs,
expecting a landmark worthy of your fame.

But then rounding a fallen headstone,
I stepped into the open and caught sight of
a family of deer seated atop a grave!
I knew at once it had to be yours.
I read your name, and the dates etched in stone,
surprised to find you'd died so young,
only fifty-seven.

As still as they were silent,
the clay sentries kept vigil
waiting, I almost heard you say, for
the sequel you never wrote.

Who put them there? I wondered.
The trio looked frozen in time, yet freshly laid.
Perhaps some diehard fan,
my antecedent, had placed the creatures there
as a tribute, a literary relic.

Too cute, you'd say. Kitsch.
As tacky as a garden gnome.
Not the right size either,
especially the fawn.
But yearlings grow quickly
as you memorably revealed.
Some die too early
by a young man's hand,
leaving a lasting mark.

Ahead of Her Time

On a fall afternoon in 1939, sparks from a pile of trash burning in the side yard ignited the roof of my grandmother's modest cottage. Gusty winds fanned the flames, and the wooden building was soon ablaze. Community volunteer firemen arrived too late and the dwelling burned to the ground, along with its contents.

In late 1923, Charlie Council moved his widowed sister Oleo Gilreath, and her five young children, from Pelham, Georgia, to the small community of Gillette, Florida, where he lived with his family.

Formal schooling ended early for many people of that era as they worked full time on family farms, or went to work in mills and factories when needed. Although Oleo's education was limited, and her employment history consisted of work in a cotton mill before her marriage, she was no stranger to hard work. The citrus groves, seasonal vegetable farming, packing houses, and a grapefruit canning plant in Gillette provided opportunities for training and employment. Oleo began grading citrus at a local packing house and she and her children soon settled into the routine of their new lives.

In 1926 Margie, the youngest child, contracted spinal meningitis. Under quarantine, Oleo cared for her at home, and she also became ill. Doctors brought in from Tampa were able to save Oleo, but Margie died. When the quarantine was lifted, officials supervised the burning or disinfecting of everything in the house.

Members of the local church took up a collection for the widow. With the proceeds of that love offering, Charlie purchased a small lot and materials and built a home for his sister and her children. Oleo moved in with two sons and her two remaining daughters.

When the house burned, my father, Leroy, and Myrtle, the eldest daughter, were already married. Myrtle and her husband lived across Tampa Bay in St. Petersburg.

After the fire, Oleo, and Aunt Omie and Blair, who were single and living at home, moved into a two-bedroom cabin at Camp Tropical, a few lots from the small rented house trailer where my parents and I lived. Near Palm View School where Omie taught grades one through three, and close to Blair's job at the feed store in Palmetto, this seemed a good place to start over.

Like many tourist courts of that time, Camp Tropical, while not luxurious, was well maintained and catered primarily to Florida's winter visitors. Four cabins with large screened porches faced Highway 41. At the rear of the property, under moss-laden grandfather oaks, ten or twelve spaces with water and electric hookups accommodated house trailers. Most of Camp Tropical's income was derived from seasonal business, but long-term rentals of a cabin or two and month-to-month rental of several park-owned trailers kept the facility open all year.

Community restrooms and showers, one side for "Gentlemen" and one side for "Ladies," were at one end of a long wooden building located in the center of the park. At the other end was a central laundry room with large, deep, wall-mounted sinks and two washing machines with hand-operated wringers. Sturdy rope clotheslines waited nearby—bring your own clothespins.

Inside the park, strips of sand spurs down the middle of gray sand roads waited patiently for my bare young feet. Try as I might, I couldn't avoid the painful stickers and I was often in tears, hobbling to find an adult to remove them.

A two-lane shell and asphalt road bordered north side of the park. One large live oak tree draped with Spanish moss, grew on a dirt island in the center of the road. The two lanes of pavement wound around opposite sides of the tree, then reconnected as the narrow roadway continued. Streets and roads in small towns and some rural areas of Florida were often paved to avoid large trees—particularly ancient oaks. Whether this was an effort to save the tree, or was simply a lazy way to avoid cutting it down, removing the stump, and carting the whole thing away is uncertain, but because of this practice, many beautiful Southern live oaks were spared in and around my home town.

Workers sometimes left a much larger area than required to bypass these trees, which had happened here, and a compact, unpainted, octagon-shaped, wooden hut shared space with the sprawling oak. For many years, passing tourists stopped there during the winter for glasses of fresh-squeezed orange juice from the adjacent groves, small jars of guava jelly, bottles of orange blossom honey, sacks of oranges to eat right away or crates of citrus to ship back home. The quaint shop closed when the main highway was rerouted and the tiny structure remained vacant for some time.

My enterprising grandmother, with no business experience and little education, was ahead of her time. The nearest grocer, where her neighbors shopped on Saturdays for their weekly supplies, was several miles away in Palmetto, so she decided to rent the tiny space and provide a "convenience store" to serve people in the trailer park and surrounding areas from Monday through Friday. Opening at 8 a.m. and staying until dusk, she quickly became successful.

The building was scarcely twelve feet across at the widest point. A long metal drink box, filled with chipped ice and bottles of Coca-Cola, Dr. Pepper, 7UP, Orange Crush, R.C., and grape and strawberry drinks, occupied much of the available space.

Each morning Grandma raised eight hefty wooden shutters that encircled the building, and latched them to the ceiling, thereby revealing a wide counter atop a wall four feet high. After sliding a cigar box containing a few bills and coins into a small drawer, and wiping the dusty countertop with a cloth dipped in frigid water from the drink box, she was open for business. Inventory space, and money for merchandise was limited so Grandma chose her stock carefully. In addition to cold drinks, she sold bread and packaged snack cakes, chewing gum, candy, cigarettes, cigars, snuff and chewing tobacco. Large glass jars filled with packaged peanut butter and cheese crackers or salted peanuts sat on the counter near bags of potato chips that were clipped to flimsy metal frames.

The first time my mother took me to Grandma's new store my heart soared. So many goodies! My not-quite-five-year-old brain immediately reasoned that my status as the only granddaughter would surely entitle me to those tempting treats whenever I wanted them. Roddy, my younger cousin, and the only other grandchild in the family lived in Orlando so I had no local competition. A practical businesswoman, Grandma just as quickly let me know that pennies and nickels were required in exchange for candy and cold drinks. I couldn't believe it. Being cute, and the only resident grandchild wasn't going to get me unlimited goodies. I was crushed!

On a shelf under the counter inside the little hut, hidden from prying eyes, were two punchboards. Although gambling was illegal in Florida, small business owners were seldom arrested for having a punchboard, but discretion was expected. Square pieces of thick cardboard or wood, punchboards contained dozens of miniature holes filled with slips of folded paper on which a number was printed. Small foil seals covered the holes to prevent cheating.

A player paid to break the seal on the hole of his choice and "punched" the slip of paper out with a wooden or metal stylus, hoping for a big win. Players were almost always men. "Ladies" didn't bet. The cost to play most punchboards was a nickel or a dime. Charts listing prizes accompanied each punchboard and winnings were often candy, cigarettes or cigars. Major brands, such as Coca-Cola and Camel cigarettes distributed punchboards with their products as prizes. Other boards specified cash amounts for winning numbers; the more expensive the play, the more valuable the listed prizes. I remember hearing grownup discussions about the long odds of winning anything worthwhile. Although most prizes were small, and winning numbers for each punchboard were few, in Florida and many other states they were the equivalent of today's lotteries and were quite popular until after WWII.

Another popular means of gambling, with higher payouts, was Bolita, a numbers game brought into Florida from Cuba in the late 1800s. Organized crime was heavily involved in running the Bolita lottery and people selling chances to that game often were arrested.

When she left in the evening, Grandma lowered the bulky shutters, latched them to the inside counter, stepped outside and padlocked the Dutch door. Although no one lived near the little building, she was never robbed, nor was there ever evidence of an attempted break-in.

On December 7, 1941, Japanese forces attacked Pearl Harbor. The country was at war and the lives of all Americans soon changed. Within weeks, Uncle Blair joined the Navy. Grandma, Aunt Omie, and my parents and I moved into town. Grandma's business venture came to an end.

The loss of her little store was a severe blow to my grandmother's budding entrepreneurship and one from which she never completely recovered. Her loss was, however, an inconsequential and unremarkable casualty of the far greater tragedy that was WWII.

Lennie Hay

Life Lines

Thirty-seven year old man
falls from moving boat
alone
miles from shore
January 2015.

School children memorized
prayers, poems, songs
believed words
strengthened them
like calisthenics
green vegetables
a daily rosary
survival lessons
January 1958.

Angel of God,
my guardian dear
to whom God's love
commits me here.

No angels near
old hands hold
today's news.

In a solitary break
from time and surf
he feels icy smack
dark foam, fears
looming death.

He treads a first
grim moment
bicycle legs move
cold water thoughts
confront sky and waves.

The Owl and the Pussy-cat went to sea
In a beautiful pea-green boat . . .

A photograph of two girls
their curls, tiny hands—
his memorized lines.
They wave just beyond
each stroke.

His wife stands solemn
lonely in his damp brain
she clings to sand years
boat days and waits.
He memorized
her lines and curves.
They buoy him.

Believe me, if all those endearing young charms,
Which I gaze on so fondly to-day . . .

Later, icy barbed wire encircles
his arms, his back stroke
each breast stroke.
Pain pierces skin
entangles
January day and night.

ODET

Daughter images dance
like rhythmic stanzas
rise and fall
fore and aft.
Tease dark choice.
Test a father's will.

Jellyfish sting.
He kicks swollen
remembers his way
through cold salt water
long darkness
led forward by family rhymes
soft evening sibilants
joyous staccato bursts.

The Lord is my shepherd . . .
He leadeth me beside the still waters,
He restoreth my soul.

Some mile past despair
a boat passes
unaware.
He stretches an ache
arches his back
and kicks, kicks.
The intimate female
verse he knows
lifts and pulls him.

Steel man
swims the Atlantic
half a day
cuts ten foot waves
covers nine miles
crawls ashore.

I never spoke with God,
Nor visited in heaven . . .

The nuns once told children
how prisoners of war
survived on memories.
Some believed.

Heat

Tupelo sat on the bench outside the Safety Harbor Post Office, where Florida's late July heat flattened the drops of sweat along his arms and chest into planes of ruin across his white shirt. His wife used to brag that she could tell the real Floridians from northern imports by their levels of effort against summer's wet heat. The more effort you exerted to resist it—from complaints against its brutality to perseverance with the absurdities of full make-up and impractical fashions—the less Floridian you were. Only when you surrendered to it could you claim to be here. He looked down at his dress shirt, his chest soaking in sweat and thick, unnecessary fabric. Well, he retorted silently, it was necessary today.

Not that Sara had been a real Floridian herself. She had moved to Tampa from Philadelphia but after a few years felt she had not only earned the title but she would not let anyone forget it, especially him.

Having been born in the Panhandle, he had found it annoying.

"Florida has seasons you know," she would respond to incoming members of the Newcomers Club where she'd met her friends for lunch just two weeks ago. "Fall is in the air," she would say in early October when the temperature dropped slightly and the water ran less slick across the air. He knew the comments weren't her, that she was imitating things she'd heard. Early in their marriage he had seen through her constructed self to the one she hid and the weaknesses that for some reason she fiercely protected. Had he called attention to them, he would have hurt her feelings and there would have been an argument, so he never had. He wasn't sure if that had made him a good husband or a bad one.

A young woman left the post office holding a baby against her chest, her sweat pressing her hair in brown lines down the sides of her face. She walked slowly, eyeing the bench as she approached. He saw in her tired eyes the quick calculation in women looking at men—will he be trouble?—before she sat beside him, falling against the cracked wood with a thump. She looked down at the baby asleep on her chest before letting her head fall back, her palm resting on the baby's head.

His cell phone rang. He ignored it, then felt an uneasy stare from the woman beside him. He picked it up.

"Tupelo?" It was Sara's sister Nancy.

"Yeah," he said.

"Are you okay? Where are you? Everyone's here."

"I'm fine," he said. "Just wanted to get out for a bit."

"Well can you come back then? We're waiting for you." She was angry.

"I know," he said. "Sorry."

"That may have worked with Sara, but you can't pull a disappearing act today. You need to get here. Now."

"I know. I'll be back."

"Look," she said, softening her tone, "you're in shock. Just come back. We can't start without you. You don't have to talk to anyone."

"I'm not in shock," he snapped. "I knew she was going to die." The woman beside him shifted and he could feel her sideways glance on him. He thought of Sara. You're at a window, she would say. The moments— beginnings and endings, losses, the shifts that bring details into high relief. It is the only time people ever really see each other, she'd said once. They had been sitting in a pew at his mother's funeral. When she said it, she had held his hand for the first time in a year, forgiving him.

"I don't mean that kind of shock," Nancy said. "I mean the *psychological* kind. It's not like being surprised."

"Fine. I'll be back soon." He ended the call and put his phone in his pocket. The young woman was watching him.

"Are you okay?" she asked. The baby whimpered.

Women sure do want to get into your head, he thought. But he could detect no hard edge. In fact, when he looked at her he had a sudden urge to put his head down. On her lap, on her chest, somewhere the hot air could press them together, make them the same in it.

"I'm okay," he said. "But thank you."

She hesitated, looked up and down Main Street as if deciding what to do.

Did he look that bad? The baby cried again. "It's okay," he added. "Really. Take care of that beautiful baby. I'll be fine."

It must have appeased her. She stood, turned back toward him and smiled. "I like your name," she said before resuming her walk down Main Street. He didn't hold her eavesdropping against her. Nancy was loud.

His name was the reason Sara had even talked to him. She and her friends had been sitting next to him at a bar in Ybor, back when the streets closed down to traffic on weekend nights until the mayor decided drunk kids were scaring away families and opened up the streets. It had angered Tupelo back in the time when there was energy to burn.

He had introduced himself to Sara as soon as she sat down.

"Tupelo, you said?" she asked, rotating her chair to see him.

"Yup," he said. "My mom worked on a honey farm."

She stared at him.

"You know, tupelo trees? Tupelo honey?"

"Oh right," she'd said. "The song!"

He laughed. "Sure, but my mom was ahead of Van Morrison."

"Well, it's a great name either way."

His mother had named him long before parents had made being unique a trend, naming their children after trees and rocks and things, names that tried so hard to be natural and original that they were neither. River, Hunter, Ashton, Forest. But that wasn't his mother. She told the story of his name as a bedtime story, the falling light glowing through the windows of their trailer to a din of cicadas, frogs and crickets, a sound that would always bring him back to summer nights with her. Back then Route 19 ran along orange groves and farmland and he had spent his days riding his bike, searching for frogs and arrowheads and swimming in lakes and inlets with the alligators before children were protected from things like predators and heat.

His mother had once worked on a tupelo honey farm on the Apalachicola River in the Panhandle, and as she told it, she had known at once that his name would "make him the kind of strong you didn't have to learn the hard way." The tupelo tree was wider at its base than at the top as if claiming its space, a broad stance across water and soil. Thriving in swamps and rivers, it could withstand hurricanes, floods, insects and rot. Not only could it absorb what would kill other honey trees, but it used the detritus and thick, humid air to produce a honey sweeter than trees in tamer climates could produce. If names had power, and his mother believed they did, she had started him off from a position of strength.

"I love it," Sara had said from her barstool. "It's like she saw your name as a blessing over your life. Do you think it has been?"

"Who knows?" he asked. "My mom was a little out there. Maybe I haven't been alive long enough to know." He was bold that night. "Maybe you can help me figure it out?"

She wrapped her hand under his elbow, hooking onto his arm playfully.

"We'll see," she said, smiling.

Well, he'd thought, sitting in heavy, watered air outside the church lobby that morning, he supposed he had lived long enough now. He was sixty-seven years old. By now you were supposed to know things, to look back on life and say what happened.

No, he thought. Anyone would agree. Too young, still too young.

The sky went gray with waiting thunderstorms. He stood, too quickly, and walked along Main Street. He passed the Paradise Restaurant, the diner that had been their staple for decades. He saw Sara sitting across from him, chicken soup and grilled cheese sandwiches, or omelets and French toast between them. Too many meals to count. It was where she liked to share news, from the mundane details of others' lives to the bombshells about theirs.

"I can't do this anymore," she'd said one night, fourteen years in. He had thought they had been sitting in amiable silence.

"What?" he asked.

"You *know* what," she'd said. She was not where he was. Again.

He figured now that it was the beginning of the same conversation every married couple had at some point, the details in the conflicts that persisted despite every effort, those you either decide to make peace with or fight to the death.

The street was nearly empty today. He stopped to rest at the dance studio, the boxy brick building where they had taken ballroom lessons a few years before. As he stared at the building, heat rose from the concrete, bending the light. He saw only waves for a moment as the building returned to what it had been: the Ellis Harbor Bank that had given them a loan for their house in 1974. Back then, with all the bars and drinkers causing trouble, the town had been nicknamed "Whiskey Harbor", and he'd had to convince Sara that $27,000 was not too much to spend for a house in a town that was on its way up. She had trusted him, and as he'd promised, the town had grown around them over the years. With it they had watched their neighbors' children, other people's children, grow from infancy to adulthood before other families replaced them. But Sara hadn't wanted to leave.

96

He shook the heat from his mind, wiped his hand across his brow and refocused his gaze. The dance studio returned. He walked up to The Stuffed Mushroom, the catering company they had used for their fortieth anniversary party. But again as he stared at the yellow pastel storefront, he felt dizzy and saw something different. This was the Grey Goose Press, he thought, where Sara had worked until it closed—four years before they'd stopped trying for good—and before she'd started working for the Colonial Florist down the road. But that was a beauty salon now, he thought. Wasn't it? He turned around and pressed forward, the heat fusing past and present in each building he passed. Floods of memory ran on water in the humid air and his mind was fluid with heat and love and pain. Past and present folded into waves of heat rising and expanding. He stared at the buildings changing before him, all of them holding outlines of Sara.

He shook his head, strained his eyes. Was the heat creating an illusion or dissolving one?

At Starbucks he thought of their recent past, hot chocolate after walks down the pier. At the pizzeria he remembered the Fourth of July, sitting on the curb with folded slices with cheese dripping onto their hands, laughter and gratitude and gladness to live here. At the Cold Stone Creamery he nearly tasted milkshakes on hot nights with their nieces, who had visited every summer for ten years. He saw in Sara's eyes the light of motherhood unexpressed, its substitute poured over the girls every moment they were here.

Which history was them, Ellis Bank or Dance Studio? Printing press or caterer? Had it been a troubled marriage or a good one?

Memories surrounded him in the heat and he felt the whirling like a sickness. He hadn't left Sara at the church. All of her was on this street.

He had to sit. He reached the library and sat on a curb outside while the rain began in drops at his feet.

The heat, he thought. Sara was right, you had to give in. Let it flatten you, pressing everything out like a sieve until only two things remained: exhaustion, the weariness itself like a certainty that you had lived, and the vague surprise that even when you just sat, it was hard, hard work. More tiring than anyone bargained for, he decided. Whatever relief you longed for—water, rest, death—you had earned it.

Oh God, he thought, it is all lived under the surface, isn't it? It was too much, the effort, the churning life of it all.

He looked up and water broke from the sky, pouring through the gaps in the thick oak trees dripping with Spanish moss over his head. Plumes of water came downward and sideways at his face soaking his shirt, dissolving the sweat against his chest.

The woman with the baby was leaving the library, running. She held an umbrella in one arm and a bag of books in the other, her baby on her hip bobbing up and down with each step, laughing. She saw Tupelo and hesitated, then ran the rest of the way to her car. She stood in the rain with her hand on the door handle. Then she opened the door, threw the books inside and closed the door before walking toward him.

"Hello again," she called. He waved a hand. She reached him and stood before him uncertainly. The rain fell in loud sheets around them. Thunder drummed across the bay.

"Look," she shouted over the storm, "I heard you say back there that someone died. And I can see you are definitely not okay." She held out her umbrella and an open palm. "Please, just let me help you."

He knew he had to get back. To the church, to everyone who loved her, to their questions and waterfalls of words and goddamned incessant how-are-yous. And he realized, his mother had been wrong about his name. There was a blessing, yes, and it was Sara. But there was no kind of strong not learned the hard way, a prize scraped out of a fight. He looked at the woman holding out her hand. What was it for her?

"Where do you need to go?" she asked. Her hand waited.

"Up the road," he said. "The Episcopal Church." It was one of the few places that had not changed hands since they had been married there forty-two years before. It would not warp in the waving water and heat that encased their history in buildings across the town.

He took the mother's hand and felt something like relief. Sara would forgive his lateness. Sara would understand. He stood, and they walked through rain and the weight of heat.

Vivian Taylor

Roadside Teddy Bear Shrine

Invisible hands arrange a plush orange and blue parrot,
faded prom portraits, a wilted floral cross, a hand-painted sign:
"Drunk Driving Kills."

I never see her—
two precarious inches of cigarette ash, Panama hat,
varicose veins below white Bermuda shorts—
styling this *momento mori* in the half light
before returning to the AstroTurf and pink flamingos of a 55+
mobile home park.

After the Summer Flowers

After the summer flowers
have faded
and when the mums
are at their peak,
in that slip of time when the world
holds it breath
for fear
of breaking the spell,

that is the dying time.

The Skull

The day started like all the others. When Henry Duncan arrived at the field, Frank Barton and Roy Jenkins were already choosing teams, Roy on account of him being the best hitter and Frank because it was his ball. The others had already been split into two groups separated by as much distance as possible, like a plateful of corn and peas.

Roy grinned his cockeyed smile when he saw the smaller boy shuffling across the grass with his scuffed-up Sears glove tucked under an armpit. "And I got Henry. Now we're even."

Everyone groaned, Frank and his squad because they were no longer up a man, and Roy's team because, well, Henry couldn't hit a lick and couldn't field any better, neither. But none of that mattered to Roy, and none of the others questioned why Henry even was allowed to play due to his tardiness. Roy stuck up for little Henry and liked having him around, though no one quite knew why, not even Roy himself.

George McAllister, who everyone called Georgie Mac, showed off his new glove, which his dad had ordered from the Wilson catalog three weeks earlier and had finally arrived from Chicago. It was made of real leather and smelled of cottonseed oil and Jimmy Foxx's name was scripted across the palm like a badge of honor. Georgie said he was up half the night breaking it in. He let the other boys touch and sniff it, but never removed it from his hand.

"Okay, let's go," Frank shouted after a few minutes. "We're up first."

Roy's boys grabbed their gloves, in some cases nothing more than threadbare lumps of leather held together by cords or torn saddle straps, and headed across the diamond, negotiating for the choicest positions.

Henry caught Roy's eye. "Right field?"

"Nah." Roy released a wad of spit into the grass. "You and me, we're gonna switch today. I'll play right."

Trying to hide his surprise, Henry nodded, pulled his red felt cap tighter over his head, and trotted toward third base.

Danny Smith, the regular shortstop since Sean Christopher disappeared the previous fall, glared. "Off the bag, numbskull! Pretend you've been there before."

Henry nodded and moved several feet to his left.

Danny grimaced, then shook his head. "Don't matter none. Just stay out of my way."

The first batter took a pitch and then hit a two-hopper directly to Danny, who gobbled it up and fired to first for the out as the rest of the team hollered, "One out!" "Two more like that one!" "Way to pitch it!"

The ball game lasted around ninety minutes, until no one had the energy to chase after a shot hit by Roy which rolled down the hill toward the mangroves along the shoreline, making the score an insurmountable 12-5. The boys tore off their shirts and headed for the diving board off the end of the pier, where the water was eight feet deep during low tide.

Roy grabbed Henry by the shoulder. "Not us," he said. "We got something else to do."

"What do you mean?"

"I wanna check out the inside of that old inn before it's too late."

Roy was referring to Carson's Baths & Resort, a sanitarium for people from up north who came to Florida for a couple of months of rest and exercise and healthy food. Carson's had gone out of business several years earlier. Since then, the building had gradually rotted away. It was rumored that the structure was going to be torn down and replaced by a restaurant.

Henry shifted his weight. "What for?"

"I want to see what's inside, is all. I heard Houdini's widow used to stay there for months, staring into her crystal ball trying to call up the dead. Other weird stuff, too." After a pause he added, "Come on. Don't chicken out on me."

"I ain't chicken."

"So let's go then." Roy reached into his pocket and pulled out a pack of Chesterfields, which he cracked open.

"Where the—where'd you get those?"

"My brother's drawer. He'll never miss 'em." Roy stuck a cigarette in his mouth and lit the end. He inhaled and coughed hard. "You ready?"

Henry glanced over his shoulder at the pier, where the rest of the boys were already swimming off the deep end. "Yeah, I guess."

Together they strolled across Bayshore and down Main Street, before turning up Second Avenue and heading north. Two blocks later they stopped in front of the old building, now overgrown with weeds, its sun-streaked paint peeling off in palm-sized flakes. A "No Trespassing" sign was staked in the yard, leaning lopsided.

Roy stole a look up and down the street before running across the grass with Henry following behind. He struck out with his foot, once, twice, before the jamb splintered apart and the door shot open with a crack.

"Come on." Roy grabbed Henry's wrist and dragged him inside, shutting the door behind them.

Thin ribbons of light streamed through the dirt-streaked windows. The room was littered with old furniture, mostly padded chairs, display cabinets, and tables made of fancy dark wood. A faded rug covered most of the floor and stank like a wet dog.

Roy strode to the counter at the far end and leaned down on one elbow. "I'd like to check in, please," he said like he was trying to imitate Cary Grant. He laughed and stubbed his cigarette on the countertop, where he left it, smoking.

"Let's get outta here," Henry pleaded. "There ain't nothing left here worth seein'."

"Not yet. I told you, I wanna look around."

Roy skirted the counter and pushed open the door behind it, which led to a dark hallway.

A small plaque with the name "Carson" was screwed to a door at the end. Roy twisted the knob and entered. The room was lit by a couple of windows partially obstructed by overgrown bushes. A certificate from the Amherst Homeopathic Institute hung over a filing cabinet. Roy removed it and tossed it into the hall, where the frame smashed apart. Then he pulled the drawers from the old desk and flung them against the walls, busting them, too.

Henry clenched his fists at his side. "What are you doing?"

Roy paused, tears welling in his eyes. "My parents are sending my brother away. To some military reform school near Tallahassee." His tone was clipped, angry.

"I'm—I'm sorry, Roy."

"It's not fair," Roy seethed. "Just not fair. He ain't done nothing wrong, nothing that no other sixteen-year-old ain't done. They say he's too much trouble and it's time he learned some responsibility."

"That stinks."

Roy stared at the ground, at the walls, at nothing. "I heard that place is dangerous."

He picked up a chair and slammed it against the floor, once, twice. "It just ain't fair. And maybe I'll be next." He swung the chair down over and over, like he was chopping firewood, until it fractured apart, leaving him holding two broken legs.

Down by his feet, the floor quivered.

"Hey—that was something." Roy got down on his knees and felt the floorboards. After a moment he looked up with a strange expression. "Check this out."

He yanked on a plank and part of the floor came up. It was a trap door, connected by a hidden hinge. Both boys leaned over and peered into the hole. Inside all was black.

"Come on," said Roy.

"I don't think we should go down there," said Henry, shaking his head. "Let's get out of here. Please, Roy. Something bad's gonna happen."

By way of response, Roy tore off his shirt, wrapped it around one of the chair legs, and lit it with a match.

"Come on." He nodded at the chair leg, now a torch. He bent his knees and jumped into the pit. "It's about five feet deep," he called up. "You better get down here. There's a tunnel. I don't know where it goes."

Henry sat down on the edge and slid into the hole. By now Roy was already moving down the corridor, his back stooped to avoid the low ceiling.

Roy held the makeshift torch in the air like Howard Carter exploring King Tut's tomb. The walls were packed dirt, but the floor felt harder, like tile. The place smelled of rats and urine.

Ahead of them was a triangle-shaped archway constructed out of stone. They continued side by side. As they passed under the arch the foul air cleared. Here the roof was higher, supported by long beams of wood that separated gold square-shaped panels, some with strange, complex symbols painted in black.

They stood straight, holding their breath. In the middle of the floor was a low podium, about waist-high, draped with a red velvet cloth. On top of this altar was a skull, glowing orange in the light of the torch. The skull faced the entrance, as if watching them.

"We shouldn't be here," Henry urged once more. "Come on, Roy. Let's get out of here."

Roy shook his head, saying nothing. He handed the torch to Henry, who took it without a word. Roy approached the altar and studied the relic. Needing both hands free, he tossed his baseball glove against the wall, where it landed next to another half-hidden in the shadows. "That looks like Sean's old mitt," he muttered. "Wonder how it got down here." He shrugged, turning his attention back to the skull in front of him.

"Leave it be," Henry said in a strange tone. "Don't touch it."

Mesmerized, Roy reached down with both hands and lifted the skull. It sparkled in the light like it was made of crystal. "Look!" he marveled, holding it close to his own head. The skull was about twice as large as his own, like it had belonged to a giant, and a round hole was cut in the back, where a woman might put her hair in a bun.

"It's some ancient Tocobaga skull," Roy continued. "Got to be. I heard they were seven feet tall. A bunch of skeletons were dug up near here in the thirties. This has got to be one of them. Must've had some secret ceremonies down here or something. Betcha that's why Houdini's widow used to come down here all the time."

Roy reached forward and ran his fingers over the smooth bone.

"I think you should put it back, Roy. It's there for a reason."

"Quit being such a baby. I'm gonna take it for a souvenir."

Roy lifted the skull, cradling it in the crook of his arm, and walked toward the archway, not noticing how Henry skirted behind him as he passed. He was halfway there when the knife sank into his back.

Roy stiffened from the pain as the skull slipped through his hands. Time stood still. The skull hit the ground and split into tiny shards, which scattered across the room like bomb fragments. Roy wheezed and gasped for breath, trying to understand.

Henry plunged the knife into his friend's back again and again, machine-like in his efficiency. Roy twisted his head around, his eyes pleading for an explanation, a reason, anything, but all he saw was Henry's pale face and sharp eyes staring back, his mouth curled into a half-smile.

"This place is sacred," said Henry, his voice emotionless. "You've disturbed things."

The knife came again. Henry noticed the symbol on Roy's ring matched one that was painted in the center of the ceiling. He tried to fight back. The torch was knocked from Henry's hand, landed in the dirt, and went out. Roy fell to his knees as he felt a new pain, this one in his right side between his ribs. He flopped forward onto his chest. His breathing stopped. All was quiet for a moment, a minute, a hundred years.

"Oh, Roy." Henry extracted the knife, wiped it on his red felt hat, and returned it to the shelf inside the altar, shutting the hidden panel afterwards. He rolled Roy's body onto its back, placed his friend's mitt under his head, and sat down in the dirt, gently stroking the older boy's cheek. "I'm sorry it had to be you." He completed the ritual killing with the words: *O-chee inhessent Manu, o-chee opdulvent Manu,* the sacrifice is due, the sacrifice is made.

Then Henry kissed his fingers and touched Roy's lips before picking up his own mitt and the now burned-out torch and passing back through the archway. He moved the familiar narrow ladder into position and climbed out of the hole, lowering the trap door behind him.

Outside, Henry walked partway down the street and rapped on the window of a one-story bungalow. An old man dressed in a flannel robe opened the door. "Yes?"

"Another's done," said Henry. "You'll have to clean it up. And fix that door again."

The man bent his head in assent, then shut the door.

Henry headed back to the marina just as the first raindrops began to fall.

"Where you been?" said Georgie Mac, slipping on his shirt. "You missed all the fun."

"Something came up," said Henry, his eyes strange. "I could use a new friend, Georgie. Will you be my friend?"

"Where's Roy?"

"He had to go. Don't think he's gonna play with us no more."

"Always knew he was good for nothin'. Come on, the storm's coming. I'll walk you home."

"Can I carry your glove?" There were those weird eyes again, somehow converting the question into an order.

Without quite knowing why, Georgie slipped his treasure off his palm. "Sure. You an' me, we're buddies now."

Express Yourself

I was doing my thing / Checking my Facebook page
just to see what's up
I came across a video / a random post
by a cyber friend who I don't even know

it was a young child / 5 or 6 years of age
he was listening to what sounded like an opera
angelic music playing in the background
and he was so caught up in the moment
he started to wave his arms / as if it was he who was conducting the music
surrounded by other well-behaved children / who were standing along his side
/ in a totally frozen pose / quiet and respectful / too afraid to show any
expression

But this kid! / He didn't care
he was lost in the moment
feeling the music / feeling his soul / feeling the soul in the music
it moved him
just as he moved it.
He was the conductor

At the end of the video
having watched this most precious of moments I thought
how limitless is the soul / it knows no time, place, or space
it is born the moment we take our very first breath and remains until
the day we escape from the plain of this existence
So what I want to say today is this:

Express yourself

Let your spirit be the guide / your spirit knows the way
it has from the instant you opened your eyes
it is the world that has robbed us of the feelings and sounds
of our soul
So we go through life letting precious moments pass us by
Lost moments / which may never return
Lost from our memory / Lost to the world
All cause / All cause
We forgot how to express ourselves
forgot how

Play in the sun / Run in the rain / See castles and dragons in the clouds
What even happened to that child
we all once knew?
So, mi gente, my people, my peeps
Sing it out / Tap it out / Shout it out!
Write it down / Record it / Video tape it! / Put a choke hold on it!
Do whatever it takes to capture the moment
Bottle it / Cork it / Save it for another time
another day and then
                                    / now here's where the real magic begins /
Come here / Right here / Same time / Every month
Come rain or shine
Whether your heart is hurting or singing
come here!
And share it with me
it could be my soul
needs to hear your moment / Your words / Your music / Jokes / Life stories
it matters not!
Just express yourself

ODET

and you don't have to be a Yeats, or Shakespeare, Elvis, or Seinfeld
those guys never lived in my world / nor don't I expect they ever would
this is our world
where I can understand you
like you understand me
so let us not let those precious moments we live
slip by because we forgot to express ourselves

                    / Share with me your world /
              your hurts and pains
          your joy and your sorrows
your fears of tomorrow

Step up to this mic / and share your world with me
                I promise you
                        it's gonna be something beautiful

CONTRIBUTORS

Holly Apperson was born in Clearwater and has called Pinellas County home ever since. Everywhere else is for adventures. She began studying her craft in high school and has continued to learn by trial and error ever since. Holly uses a Nikon to capture her love of nature, but she is always eager to explore new subject matter. Her work has been published in promotional advertisements, a corporate calendar, and included in the book *A Brief History of Safety Harbor, Florida*. She has also won contests for her work.

Walt Belcher is a former TV critic and feature writer for *The Tampa Tribune* for nearly 35 years. He taught writing for mass communications at The University of Tampa. After nearly 35 years in Hillsborough County Walt and his wife Debbie moved to downtown Safety Harbor to enjoy the art, music and culture the area has to offer. Still writing daily for pleasure, he also spends time with five grandkids and his two sons and their families.

As a woman of color, **Amy Bryant**'s life has been shaped by a multicultural mosaic, spanning Europe, Africa and the Caribbean. Her memoir, *You CAN Go Home Again: Reflections of a Nubian Daughter,* is a collection of vignettes to honor the richness of a heritage that defines her unique American experience. A retired psychotherapist, Amy currently blogs for *Safety Harbor Connect.*

Gregory Byrd's prose has appeared in the *St. Petersburg Times, Good Old Boat, American Motorcyclist* and elsewhere. His poems have appeared widely in journals in the United States and abroad. His latest book of poems is *Salt and Iron* (Snake Nation, 2014). Among his awards are a Creative Pinellas Rapid Returns Fellowship, Fulbright Fellowship to Albania, and a Pushcart Prize Nomination. He teaches writing and humanities at St. Petersburg College.

A Florida native and retiree, **Patricia Daharsh** writes haiku and records memories of her childhood travels throughout the eastern U.S. with migrant parents. Non-fiction has appeared in *Pinesong, The Seven Hills Review* and *Cuirve River VII.* In 2009 & 2015 Pat's entries placed First in the ukiaHaiku International competition. Additional prose and haiku entries have been finalists in national and international contests. She is working on a memoir.

Bruce Duncan has worn many hats over the years: architect, real estate developer, primary parent, urban planner, and, always, photographer. Bruce has taken classes at the Provincetown Arts Center, and his work has been recognized at the Indian Rocks

Beach Art Center and the Tarpon Springs Art Contest. While he seeks interesting structural details, animals, and street photography, he loves experimenting with his photos to make the hidden visible.

The managing editor of *Odet*, **Warren Firschein** is the author of *Out of Synch* and the coauthor of *A Brief History of Safety Harbor, Florida*. A graduate of the University of Pittsburgh School of Law, where he served as an editor of the University of Pittsburgh Law Review, and Carnegie Mellon University's Tepper School of Business, he is a long-time attorney for the Federal Communications Commission. He lives in Safety Harbor, Florida, with his wife and two daughters.

Michelle Glans is a twelfth-grade student in the Creative Writing and Visual Arts departments at Miami Arts Charter School. She has been published in *Creative Communications* and the *Young American Poetry Digest*, and has won two gold keys in Scholastics Art and Writing as well as three silver keys. She lives in Miami with her parents.

A former advertising art director and graphic artist, **Carrie Font Granato** now fulfills her creative needs through writing prose. She is currently at work on two light romance novels, which draw upon her Cuban heritage. When not creating, she can be found teaching karate, practicing yoga, and enjoying nature along Florida's Gulf Coast. She is the art director and an editor of *Odet*.

Daniela Gutierrez lives in Miami with her mom and her sister. She attends Miami Arts Charter under the Creative Writing branch. When she grows up, she hopes to combine her passion for history and writing.

After 42 years in education, **Lennie Hay** now uses her life-long love of language and her energy to write poetry. She draws on her love of music, family history, foreign travel, and the sound of the surf washing up on the beach of Indian Shores, where she now lives with her husband Bruce Duncan, as subjects for her poetry. Recently Lennie entered the low-residency MFA program at Spalding University in Louisville, KY.

Maureen Jenkins is a playwright and poet. She is part of the Poetry Circle at OLLI at Eckerd College in St. Petersburg, Florida, a member of the Dramatists Guild, Suncoast Playwrights and Pinellas Writers. She lives in Largo, FL and Pittsburgh, PA.

Jeff Jeter is a Florida native and former member of the FFA, NRA and American Mensa. Jeff holds a full-time job and barbecues when he can. His interests include responsible parenthood, malty ales and sketching caricatures during staff meetings. His work has been published in *Solo Novo* and *The Sandhill Review.*

Jen Karetnick is the author of three full-length collections of poetry, including *American Sentencing* (Winter Goose Publications, May 2016) and *The Treasures That Prevail* (Whitepoint Press, September 2016), as well as four poetry chapbooks. Her work has appeared recently or is forthcoming in *Negative Capability, One, Painted Bride Quarterly, Prairie Schooner Review, Spillway* and *Verse Daily*. She works as the Creative Writing Director for Miami Arts Charter School and as a freelance dining critic, lifestyle journalist and cookbook author.

Katherine Kennedy is a teacher, writer and college advisor. She holds graduate degrees in Education from American University and Harvard University. She lives with her husband and three children in their adopted hometown of Sarasota, Florida.

Ariana Kepner (illustrations) graduated from USF with a Bachelor's in Anthropology. She lives in Safety Harbor and enjoys a wide range of subjects, often discovered through books. In her spare time she draws, paints and creates whimsical creatures in paper maché. A previous illustration was included in *A Brief History of Safety Harbor, Florida*.

Wendy Keppley, a Florida native, counseled troubled teens and taught college courses for high school honor students. She enjoys family, playing with her grandsons, and living in the woods near Tampa. Wendy also loves writing, kayaking, reading, yoga, exploring waterfalls, and oneirology.

After years as an IT professional, **P. R. King** is currently focused on writing fiction. Her current project is a mystery novel which, coincidentally, takes place in a condo community on Florida's Gulf coast. She has completed a Middle Grade novel based on her childhood experience of living in Libya. She's an avid reader, currently obsessed with the Harry Bosch series. She is impatient and stubborn which she blames on her moon being stuck in Capricorn.

Darla Klein has previously published poetry in *Friends Journal, Melting Trees Review*, and in *Tulip Trees Review* as recipient of an Honorable Mention in their *Stories That Need to Be Told* Contest. She lives in Clearwater and is inspired by both sunny beach days and ferocious thunderstorms. If she's not journaling on her patio, she might be seen performing at an open mic, off in the woods camping, or in silent retreat.

Deborah Klein has been a resident of Safety Harbor for several years. She is a blogger and a poet and was awarded best local poet for 2016 by *Creative Loafing*. She is a member of the Safety Harbor Writers & Poets as well as the Safety Harbor Art and Music Collective. Deborah shares her little home with two cats and a vortex somewhere in the kitchen. She has a daughter who lives in San Francisco.

Romeo Lemay was born in Quebec, Canada and passed away at the age of 89 in Palm Harbor, Florida. At a young age, Romeo was a Cub Reporter for *LeDroit*, a French newspaper. He joined General Motors of Canada in 1946 and retired at 58 with 37 years of service as Lead Hand in the Master Mechanic Division of the Precision Tool Grinding Division. While at G.M. he was co-editor for the 199 News for the UAW plant union and others affiliated in the area. Romeo had been encouraged by family and friends to write down his stories, and fortunately, he did. His self-published book, *Facts Fiction, Fantasies and Foolishness* has allowed for his humor and wit to live on. While he is greatly missed by his friends and family, a scholarship allows them to introduce him to others through an annual writing contest in his name.

Andrea McBride relocated to the Tampa area from Ohio in 2009. She discovered a love for poetry after joining the Writers' Circle from Saint Leo University in San Antonio, Florida. She has had poems published in several journals including *Alba*, *A Handful of Stones*, *River Poets*, and the *Sandhill Review*.

Cameron Hunt McNabb is an assistant professor of English at Southeastern University in Lakeland, FL and a fourth-generation Florida native. Her work focuses on her home state and has appeared or is forthcoming in journals such as the *Tampa Review Online*, *Steel Toe Review*, *Neutrons Protons*, *Creative Loafing*, and *Deep South*.

Marcia Jaron Morley is a former journalist and visiting instructor in English at Purdue University. She was the recipient of several poetry and prose awards while at Purdue and has had work published in magazines and newspapers. A transplanted Hoosier, she loves living in beautiful Florida, which inspires her poetry and fiction. Marci resides in Clearwater with her husband, Jack.

A closet poet for many years, **Louise Moses** recently entered the world of submissions where she enjoys occasional encouragement. A theoretical mathematician by training, she was born in Ohio, lives in Florida, and aspires to live in Paris.

Kaitlin Murphy-Knudsen is a writer, editor and writing coach who lives in Safety Harbor, Florida. Her work has appeared in Newsweek, The Washington Post, Condé Nast Traveler and other national publications. She also ghostwrites for individuals and non-profit organizations, and she has taught writing at The University of Tampa, American University, Buffalo State College, and secondary schools in the United States and Japan. She holds a bachelor's degree from Columbia University and a master's in Secondary English Education from New York University.

Katherine Nichols was born in Miami and attended Miami Arts Charter School where she double majored in Photography and Creative Writing. She enjoys writing poetry and non-fiction. Katherine received a National Gold Medal in Scholastic Art and Writing and she was published in the Susquehanna Journal. In addition to her arts, she loves traveling and meeting new people.

Dianne Persall is a 27-year resident of the Tampa Bay area and a slow but enthusiastic triathlete. She is a member of the Story Circle Creative Writing Group and has been published in the last three Safety Harbor Story Circle Annual chapbooks.

After majoring in Literature at Yale, **Brooks Peters** worked as a freelance writer and editor in New York, contributing to *Architectural Digest, Opera News, Metropolitan Home, OUT, Quest,* and *Vanity Fair.* Since moving to Florida he has pursued a new passion: poetry. In 2016 he won first prize in *Creative Loafing*'s Poetry contest.

Carlos Rolon (known to his friends as Chino), has been writing spoken word since 1975. As he puts it, he cut his poetic teeth at the place called the Nuyorican Poets Cafe in NYC. The cafe was founded by writer and poet Miguel Algarin in 1973. It started and created a new movement called Nuyorican Poetry. Chino is now a resident of Tampa and continues to perform spoken word at open mics throughout the tri-city area.

Laurie Ross, fine art photographer, lives, plays and works in her hometown of St. Petersburg, Florida. Locally renowned for her 2013 book, *Shop Dogs: A Photo Essay of Dogs That Go To Work.* Laurie brings nearly 30 years of experience to her work, which also includes events such as parties, smaller weddings, portraits, and other intimate occasions that allow her freedom to express her artistic vision.

Born in England, **Camilla Shoosmith** emigrated to Florida as a child, spending much of her childhood in the sunshine. She is a graduate of Boca Ciega High School and has a Bachelor's in Biology from the University of South Florida. She is currently studying Secondary Science Education at St. Petersburg College. In her free time, you can find her with her husband and her daughter, or of course, writing.

Elisa Silverstein is an 11th grade student from Miami. She is currently taking creative writing in school and she enjoys writing poetry, short stories, and songs.

Noah Snitzer is a Junior in Miami Arts Charter school. He has won multiple awards, including two gold keys for poetry and flash-fiction in Scholastics, and a national silver medal. In his free time, he reads, enjoys the warm shores of Miami, and watches funny animal videos.

Jason Swierk lives in Safety Harbor and is proud to be part of the city's vibrant writing and arts community. He is currently seeking representation for his novel and is pursuing journals for his shorter works.

Vivian Taylor, PhD, finished her first novel on New Year's Eve then watched fireworks over water. Poet, theorist, editor, writer, freelancer. Taylor's bylines appear in Tributary, Saw Palm, Journal of Critical Animal Studies, German Cinema: A Critical Filmography to 1945, etc., and her uncredited oeuvre is broader and as diverse.

Jaclyn Telfair graduated from the University of Florida with a degree in Animal Biology. Since 2006, she has worked as a government scientist in Tampa. When not in the laboratory, she spends her time writing, drawing, or making wine. The hours spent running on Florida trails helps fuel her imagination.

Elyse Thomas is an 8th grade writer from the creative writing department in Miami Arts Charter School. She has been published three times so far in several poetry anthologies and participated in Piano Slam 8 by performing in the Adrienne Arsht Center. Elyse continues to write and work on her craft. She hopes to gain more opportunities to elevate and present her writing in the near future.

Terrie Dahl Thomas is from Warren, Pennsylvania, and graduated from Edinboro University with a degree in Geography with a focus in Environmental Planning. Her family moved to Safety Harbor in 1983 and Terrie joined them in 1991. Terrie loves capturing the beauty of nature through both photography and Gyotaku, the ancient Japanese art of fish rubbing. Terrie's photography has been featured on NOAA's World Ocean Day's photography challenges and also in the book, *A Brief History of Safety Harbor, Florida*. Terrie's favorite thing to do is explore outdoors with her husband Chip and daughter Fairl, camera in hand.

Cheryl A. Van Beek is grateful to be published in the first issue of *Odet* and also to have had poems published with *Creative Writing Ink, Sandhill Review, River Poets Journal* and many others. She has also written for a local newspaper. She lives with her wonderful husband and their two cats in Florida, "The Land of Flowers."

Alaina Virgilio is a local freelance photographer residing near the historic town of Tarpon Springs. She is 27 years old and likes a good book, coffee, and getting behind her camera. She uses her skills to create images that evoke both emotion and wonder. A creative outlet to break through the mundane.

Resie Waechter is a St. Pete native who is currently studying English and History at the University of South Florida. She loves finding hidden gems in the city, and exploring everything Florida has to offer.

Janet Watson, who was born in Ohio, has called Florida home for many years, and currently resides in Pasco County. Her poetry has been published in anthologies and literary journals, and in her book *Eyes Open, Listening.* She is Youth and Student Contest Chair for the Florida State Poets Association and is president of New River Poets, a local chapter of that organization.

William L. Willard, Sr. has been writing for and about traditional Americans for over 40 years. Born in New York City in 1946, he enlisted in the Air Force in 1964 and was assigned to Hickam AFB, Hawaii, where he met Sue Ann Davis. They married in 1969 and still are. The Willards have lived in Tampa Bay since 1985.